UNIVERSITY OF
WOLVERHAMPTON
KNOWLEDGE • INNOVATION • ENTERPRISE

Harrison Learning Centre
City Campus
University of Wolverhampton
St Peter's Square
Wolverhampton WV1 1RH
Telephone: 0845 408 1631
Online Renewals:
www.wlv.ac.uk/lib/myaccount

Telephone Renewals: 01902 321333 or 0845 408 1631
Online Renewals: www.wlv.ac.uk/lib/myaccount
Please return this item on or before the last date shown above.
Fines will be charged if items are returned late.
See tariff of fines displayed at the Counter.

Western Capitalism and State Socialism

Western Capitalism
and
State Socialism

An Introduction

HOWARD DAVIS AND RICHARD SCASE

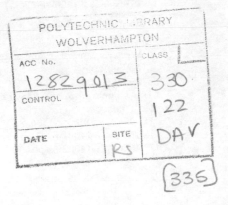
Basil Blackwell

© Howard Davis and Richard Scase 1985

First published 1985

Basil Blackwell Ltd
108 Cowley Road, Oxford OX4 1JF, UK

Basil Blackwell Inc.
432 Park Avenue South, Suite 1505,
New York, NY 10016, USA

British Library Cataloguing in Publication Data

Davis, Howard
   Western capitalism and state socialism:
   an introduction.
   1. Socialism   2. Capitalism
   I. Title   II. Scase, Richard
   330.12'2   HX72
   ISBN 0-631-14001-8
   ISBN 0-631-14002-6 (Pbk.)

Library of Congress Cataloging in Publication Data

Davis, Howard.
   Western capitalism and state socialism.
   Bibliography: p.
   Includes index.
   1. Communism.   2. Capitalism.   I. Scase, Richard.
   II. Title.
   HX73.D38 1985   335.5   85-9230
   ISBN 0-631-14001-8
   ISBN 0-631-14002-6 (pbk.)

Typeset by System 4 Associates, Gerrards Cross, Bucks.
Printed in Great Britain by Billings Ltd, Worcester

Contents

Preface

This book is derived from one of our undergraduate courses which we jointly teach at the University of Kent at Canterbury. We are grateful to the students who, through the years, have enthusiastically contributed to the clarification of many of our ideas and arguments. We also thank Sue Steele who kindly typed the various drafts of this book, and Jane Benson who prepared figure 2.

H.D.
R.S.

Introduction

This book is intended as a brief introduction to the study of Western capitalist and East European state socialist societies. There is no attempt to offer new theories and explanations. Our aim is more modest; to review each of these types of society so that the student may obtain a better understanding of their similarities and differences. Indeed, it is only since the 1960s that Western capitalist and East European state socialist countries have been viewed as distinctive social types. Before then, there was a tendency to regard the Soviet Union and many other countries in Eastern Europe as 'deviant' and 'social pathological', countries which would be fundamentally changed either by the 'inherent' forces of industrialism or by active political struggle (Dahrendorf, 1959; Kerr et al., 1960). Since the 1960s, however, it has become increasingly recognised that the countries of Eastern Europe possess structural characteristics which clearly differentiate them from their Western counterparts. Even so, the precise character of these differences remains problematic and the very nature of these countries continues to remain the focus for considerable debate.

Before the creation of the Soviet Union in 1917 and the emergence of East European state socialist countries during the 1940s, sociological observers were concerned primarily to identify the key features of industrial society.[1] While some focused upon the emergence of new forms of work, others were preoccupied with the dislocating effects which the industrialisation process was having upon traditional patterns of social relationships. Thus there has often been a contradictory attitude towards industrialisation among sociologists, with many being unable to decide whether or not the growth of industrial society constitutes genuine human progesss. The greater material rewards and the general improvement in living standards which industrialisation has brought for large numbers of people have often been contrasted with the ways in which modern technology has reinforced the exploitative nature of work relationships and the world's vulnerability to destruction through military confrontation. At the same time, the growth of industrial society has encouraged a general acceptance of technological change and a view that human beings are powerless to halt the forces of scientific and technical progress. In many ways, modern technology has acquired the status of a 'god' whose forces are beyond human control.

If, then, there has been and remains a general ambivalence towards the merits of industrial and technological change – and this has been reflected in the perspectives of different social observers – modern technology has been regarded as more popular at some points of time than at others. Perhaps in the mid-1980s, it is rather less popular than in the 1950s and the 1960s. During those earlier decades there was widespread optimism about the direction of technological development, since it was seen to offer solutions to many age-old human problems. Indeed, during the immediate post-war era industrialism was regarded as possessing an inner 'logic' which was capable of transforming the socio-political structures of different societies (Kerr et al., 1960). It was argued that as countries became more industrialised they also became more democratic, egalitarian and pluralistic in their power structures. Further, it was often alleged that the industrialisation process brought about the erosion of traditional class structures within which social positions were ascribed, to be replaced by more 'open' and 'meritocratic' social systems. Similarly, it was claimed that old-style class conflicts were being eroded, to be superseded by negotiation among institutionally prescribed pressure groups which, according to the 'rules of the game', determined the allocation of resources in society (Dahrendorf, 1959). In the 1950s and 1960s, therefore, there was a strongly held view that industrial societies were, because of inherent forces associated with industrial change, becoming more egalitarian, open and democratic. It was even held that the 'totalitarian' regimes of many developing and Eastern European countries would ultimately collapse because of their inability to resist socio-political changes brought about by the development of industrial society.

Indeed, the optimism of such views was reflected in the claims that 'industrialism' would ultimately evolve into 'post-industrialism' (Bell, 1973). Factories would give way to offices, and traditional forms of manufacturing to either 'high' technology or the provision of various kinds of services. Further, in the post-industrial society, the quest for profit would be superseded by the predominance of welfare ideologies which would stress the need for cooperation rather than competition. In such a society, the planners, the technocrats and the scientific workers would be the leaders and the technologically advanced research establishments the 'key' institutions. The post-industrial society, then, was seen to express the ultimate in human progress and it was regarded as the logical outcome of processes which were set in motion during the industrial revolution of the late eighteenth and early nineteenth centuries. Such a society, in other words, was deemed to be on the verge of achieving the ultimate goal of the industrialisation process; social harmony and material affluence, and the abolition of conflict and deprivation. If there were going to be problems in such a society, these – so it was held – could be ameliorated within the parameters of postindustrialism by 'fine tuning' according to the prescriptions of social, economic and technical planners.

However, this almost universal belief in the benefits of industrialism and post-industrialism became increasingly challenged once living standards ceased to improve at the rate experienced during the 1960s. The lack of growth in the Western economies during the 1970s and 1980s led to a fundamental reappraisal of the alleged desirable features of post-war industrialism, and its more 'ugly' side attracted greater attention. An attractive view of large-scale organisations was replaced by claims that they consisted of cumbersome bureaucratic procedures, enhancing feelings of personal powerlesssness and curtailing human creativity (Schumacher, 1973). These same organisations were increasingly seen to be socially irresponsible, since their owners and/or managers were rarely accountable to employees and to the communities and regions within which they were located. They were often seen to be making excessive claims upon the world's resources for the production of goods and services which many considered to be of highly questionable value (Dickson, 1974). Add concerns about environmental pollution and the exploitation by Western corporations of many third-world countries and the scene was set for a fundamental reappraisal of the virtues of post-war industrialism.

Increasingly, individuals responded to these processes not in terms of widespread political protest but in more 'individual' and 'private' ways. Although there has been the growing popularity of the Green Party in Western Germany, the increasing attractiveness of small-scale organisations as places for employment, and a greater concern for environmental matters in general, the failure of economic growth and the increasing frustrations associated with modern urban–industrial living have been most commonly expressed by a 'retreat' into the private world of family and personal relationships. People in the present-day Western world have become more and more cynical about the effectiveness of the institutions which control their lives and about the extent to which these can improve the quality of life. If, then, industrialism in the 1950s and the 1960s was the expression of enlightened social change, in the conditions of the 1980s the institutions of industrial society are increasingly seen to inhibit the capacity for human progress.

However, such views of industrialism are misplaced. This is because such discussions describe little and explain even less. This is not only because of a number of fundamental issues associated with definition but also because 'industrialism' is a catch-all term which is both ambiguous and imprecise in its meaning. In the final analysis, what *does* industrialism mean apart from its use as a general term to describe the differences between 'industrial' and 'non-industrial' countries? If some definitions refer to inanimate, technological processes, others refer not only to technology but to a wider range of social and economic variables. (If, for some writers, industrialism refers to a system of technological processes, for others it describes 'ways of life' and societies in general.) As a result, it is difficult to determine cause-and-effect relationships because of the cluster of factors which constitute the nature of the industrial process.

Further, and associated with this, an emphasis upon 'technological change' implies a form of determinism which is questionable. Patterns of industrial and technological change become 'decontextualised' from the wider socio-political processes which shape their direction. How else can research and development in the aerospace industries, the military manufacturing establishments and the medical research laboratories be explained other than by reference to their sponsorship by either state or privately owned corporations (Melman, 1970)? In other words, a preoccupation with industrialism, technology and scientific progress – and they are closely interrelated in the popular mind – detracts from an understanding of the *real* sources of power in modern society. Behind every scientist and research worker there are politicians, ministers and shareholders. It is they, rather than any inherent logic of industrialism, who shape the direction of technological and scientific change.

The determining effects of modern technology were most strongly emphasised during the immediate post-war decades when the position of a number of Eastern European regimes became consolidated. During this period, it was often argued that the effects of industrialism were such that two processes would ultimately occur. First, it would bring about the destruction of totalitarianism. Secondly, it would bring about a convergence of state socialist and Western capitalist countries (Galbraith, 1967; Kerr et al., 1960; Lipset, 1960). According to such arguments, as these societies industrialised, they would develop similar occupational structures, institutional orders, stratification systems, patterns of privilege and reward, and pluralistic power structures within which interest groups would bargain over the allocation of resources. Consequently, the totalitarian regimes of Eastern Europe were seen as nothing more than temporary features on the European landscape: with the ever-increasing impact of the industrialisation process, they would inevitably become more 'open' and 'democratic', taking on the features of all modern industrial countries.

Two decades later, such claims seem absurd. As the military build-up between East and West continues and as the regimes of Eastern Europe retain their repressive and totalitarian characteristics, it is difficult to identify a pattern of convergence between East and West European countries. Indeed, the nature and form of social conflict in these societies, the manner in which each is prone to rather different forms of crisis and the ways in which each is responding to the world economic recession of the 1980s confirm the extent to which there are fundamental differences between them. Even if both types of society reflect similarities in their urban–industrial patterns of living, such features are superficial by comparison with their more fundamental and striking differences. In order to understand these, we need to recognise that the countries of Eastern and Western Europe are the expression of forces inherent within their respective modes of production.

Many writers, of course, rebut the contention that the mode of production differs in East and Western Europe. On the contrary, they argue that it is impossible to make as simple a contrast and that *within* both East and Western Europe there are countries with highly varied socio-political forms. (Such is the approach of many political scientists who, by comparison with sociologists, are often more concerned with the national specificity of political institutions and processes.) They contend that, even if we overlook these, the *nature* of the countries that make up East and Western Europe is problematic and warrants further clarification. Certainly, there is considerable debate about the nature of the East European countries. For those who focus upon political processes, the structure of political institutions and the procedures whereby societal decisions are taken, such countries are regarded as inherently *totalitarian* (Friedrich and Brzezinski, 1965). According to this view, there are no legitimate channels through which the grievances of subordinate groups may be expressed, if only because the Communist Party monopolises all channels of communication within society. Any challenge to the authority of the Party is perceived as illegitimate and, by definition, as counter-revolutionary, inspired by a desire to undermine the established socio-political order. Consequently, the totalitarian nature of these countries is underscored by a variety of coercive institutions and by a normative consensus which restricts debate, encourages political acquiescence and reinforces the monopoly dominance of the Party and the state machinery. In Poland, for instance, the Party regards Solidarity as counter-revolutionary because it directly challenges the legitimacy of the Party and its self-acclaimed right to direct the future of society in the name of, and for the good of, the people.

Such a view of East European countries is often closely related to claims that they are somehow *degenerate* and *bureaucratic* in their nature (Djilas, 1966). Such an approach argues that state bureaucratic structures have emerged which no longer represent the interests of the working classes. Instead, officials exploit the various bureaucratic state apparatuses for the purposes of personal gain and for attaining goals which give them privileges compared with other groups. Their control over planning processes relating to the production and allocation of resources – for example, health and educational services, housing, and the provision of various consumer goods – ensures that their material living conditions are superior to those of other groups in society (Szelenyi, 1983). Consequently, it is argued that social and economic inequalities are increasing in a number of East European countries. Despite this, there is little working-class protest; any such action would be perceived as anti-state or anti-Party, its purpose to undermine the goals of society as a whole.

It is further argued that the essentially bureaucratic character of these countries is compounded by an excessive reliance upon rules and procedures which regulate all aspects of economic and social life. Hence, the organisation and direction of society according to 'plans' means that there are inevitably cumbersome procedures for decision-making and that the provision of goods and services will rarely meet consumer demand in an efficient and rational manner – at least by comparison with the ways in which the market operates to determine the allocation of resources in Western capitalist countries. For many writers, therefore, East European countries are essentially bureaucratic and, as a result, they are characterised by ruling strata which enjoy all manner of privileges and, at the same time, retain a firm grip over society through their control over the planning process. Consequently, according to this view, these societies are prone to corruption, the abuse of power and the inefficient allocation of resources. Further, they are inclined to deep-rooted structural conflicts between privileged strata of bureaucrats and Party officials on the one hand and the producers of economic wealth on the other. Such conflicts will persist, so it is claimed, until the privileged and degenerate bureaucratic apparatus is dismantled and a political process is instigated within which all groups will be represented and the Party and state officials made directly accountable to the broad mass of people.

A contrasting view is that East European countries are essentially *state capitalist* (Cliff, 1974). Such an approach dwells upon the material bases of these countries rather than upon their political or ideological systems. According to this view, there is little difference between the nature of the productive processes in Eastern and

Western European countries. Both are capitalist in their overall
exploitative features and the only difference between them is in their
ownership function. Whereas the state is the owner of the productive
system in East European countries, in the West ownership is
exercised by a variety of individual and institutional shareholders.
But, in both types of society, the productive process is characterised
by exploitative relationships according to which the economic
surplus created by the producers is expropriated by managers,
controllers and the owners of productive enterprises. Thus there
are few institutional differences between East European and Western
capitalist countries – particularly in their economic enterprises
– since both are characterised by exploitative and antagonistic
relationships and both are geared to the production of goods and
services for profit. Consequently, they possess similarities in their
technical divisions of labour, patterns of industrial discipline and
the factory systems required for profitable production.[2] Each type
of society, therefore, creates similar forms of conflict because of
common features in their productive systems.

If there are major contrasts between the two types of society,
they are in the absence of 'free' trades unions in Eastern Europe
and the way in which production takes place under a form of political
totalitarianism unlike the more open system of representative
democracy in the West. Even so, many observers claim that such
differences should not be overstated if only because the so-called
democratic processes of the West operate within systems which
generate glaring socio-economic and political forms of inequality,
so that representative democracy is often more illusory than real.
In other words, the work, living and educational experiences of
many sectors of the working class are such that their participation
within the political process is minimal and may consist of little more
than casting votes at the occasional general election.

For the theorists of state capitalism, therefore, the solution to
the problems of East European countries is the same as for the
countries of the West; revolution. Such writers argue that the
contradictions in Eastern Europe will become more acute as the
capitalist mode of production continues to develop and revolution
will be required if the exploitative features of these countries are
to be abolished. Only then can a more authentic form of socialism
be introduced according to which the planning process will be

geared to the general needs of the population rather than to implicit or explicit measures of profitability (Cliff, 1974).

If there is debate over the nature of East European countries, there is comparable dispute over the character of Western countries. As we have already suggested, the view of these societies as 'post-industrial' is often put forward on the ground that these countries have changed fundamentally in their productive systems during the course of the twentieth century. This is because there has been a shift from the production of manufactured goods to the provision of services and 'high' technological products during the post-war era (Bell, 1973). But, in our view, such changes do not really warrant a 'new label' if only because the motive underlying the production of goods and services is, as ever, the quest for profit and for capital accumulation. Western societies are as capitalist in their nature as they have ever been and even the growth of state-financed systems of welfare provision should not detract from this. Accordingly, we reject claims that Western countries have become 'post-capitalist' or 'welfare capitalist' and, as such, display features which distinguish them from their earlier forms.

Any large-scale changes which may have occurred over the past two hundred years – and there have, of course, been many – have not substantially eroded the underlying principle according to which the production of goods and services is organised. The scale of capitalist production may be greater today in that it transcends national boundaries, and national states may directly intervene in privately owned economies to a larger extent than in the past, but in the final analysis it is the production of goods and servcies for profit which constitutes the core around which capitalist society is organised.[3]

For the purposes of writing this introductory book, then, we begin with the assumption that there are fundamental differences between the countries of Eastern Europe and the Western world. Accordingly, to describe these societies as simply *industrial* is to detract from a number of their more striking contrasts. Indeed, each is characterised by a distinctive mode of production which accounts for the ways in which each is responding to the conditions of the 1980s. If the countries of the West can be regarded as essentially capitalist, the countries of Eastern Europe can be viewed as overwhelmingly state socialist. They may possess various bureaucratic and totalitarian attributes, but these, in our view, can only be understood by reference to their more general features as state socialist countries. The claim that they are state capitalist can be rejected because such a view is so evidently wrong. There is, for instance, no stock exchange in the Soviet Union; capital assets cannot be purchased, sold and transmitted within generations of families as they can be in the West. Economic enterprises cannot shift their sites of production to low-wage economies in the manner of Western corporations and there are none of the propertied rentiers that are so prevalent in Western countries. For these and many other reasons, we hold the view that Eastern European countries should be viewed as state socialist and that they operate, as such, according to processes which are vitally different to those in the West.[4]

It is only by reference to differences in their modes of production that it is possible to understand the ways in which the countries of Eastern Europe and of the Western world are adapting to a variety of worldwide problems in the closing decades of the twentieth century. East European countries possess the greater capacity to handle the problems of economic depression, unemployment and the general process of deindustrialisation. On the other hand, the socio-political organisation of these countries is often repressive and limits personal freedom to an extent which large numbers of people in the Western world regard as intolerable. The capitalist countries, by contrast, are less able to cope with the problems of economic recession and industrial decline if only because jobs and occupations are determined by profit-making corporations. They are, then, less able to plan for employment on the basis of need, social contribution, and criteria of human creativity. So economic hardship is likely to be experienced by increasing numbers of people in the Western world during the closing decades of the twentieth century. At the same time, however, capitalist corporations do not exercise an all-embracing control over citizens in the manner of the state in East European countries. Consequently, both types of society are faced with crises during the remainder of the twentieth century but if the nature of this in Eastern Europe is *political*, in the advanced Western countries, it is of a more *economic* kind. We now turn our attention to the reasons for this, beginning with an analysis of the development of capitalist society.

Part I

The Analysis of Western Capitalism

1

The Development of
Capitalist Society

The origins of the social sciences, and particularly those of sociology, are to be found in the emergence of industrial capitalism as a socio-economic system. New patterns of work and living in Europe during the eighteenth and nineteenth centuries convinced many observers of the need for a scientific study of these processes. The so-called 'founding fathers' of modern sociology – especially Karl Marx, Max Weber and Emile Durkheim – shared a common interest in the growth of the factory system and in the mechanisms of social order and change.[1] On the basis of observation and measurement, they sought to identify structured regularities in social behaviour, institutions and societies. They argued that these patterns could be explained by cause-and-effect relationships which, in turn, may be expressed in terms of 'laws' of social development.[2]

They were concerned with these problems not for purely theoretical reasons but because they felt that industrialisation was creating social pressures which only scientific analysis could resolve. They were witness to dramatic changes which were destroying traditional institutions, patterns of behaviour and values. During the nineteenth century, the basis of social order seemed to be threatened and they held that a major task for a science of society was to resolve the problems created by industrialisation (Durkheim, 1964). These early sociologists argued that the laws governing patterns of social order and change could only be established on the basis of the historical and comparative study of institutions and social structures (Weber, 1964). Above all, they attempted to grasp the nature of indus-trialisation as a general process which was creating fairly uniform effects in countries with contrasting traditions and institutions. For example Marx, Weber and Durkheim each produced classifications of pre-industrial and industrial societies in order to interpret the dynamics of social change. It was within this broad comparative perspective that they attempted to identify the major characteristics of the newly emerging industrial order.

One of the key features of the emerging industrial capitalism was the entrepreneur who organised the manufacture and sale of commodities for profit. Under this system, goods and services were no longer produced solely to meet basic needs, as for example in the family or guild systems, but in such a way that proprietors could obtain profits from selling in the market. Generally speaking, until the industrial revolution, the manufacture of most goods was for local demand – for example, clothing, furniture, technical implements, utensils, etc. – and was predominantly undertaken in households within which there was the exercise of traditional artisan skills, simply organised among family members. In contrast, capitalist entrepreneurs produced commodities which not only were manufactured for direct consumption but were created for the purposes of monetary exchange in the market.

Capital accumulation through profit, then, became the overriding motive for the production of goods. This, in turn, shaped all aspects of work – for example, the nature of the relationship between employers and employees; the adoption of new technologies; the specification of job tasks and the general conditions under which goods were produced. Thus production of goods for a *profit* was the basis for the economically rational factory system. As we shall see later, it was not mechanical innovation *per se* which brought about the factory system; rather, the growth of factories was a response to a number of organisational problems associated with the drive for profitability. The production of woollen garments, for example, does not require factories; these only become necessary when owners compete with each other to sell their wares in markets for profit. Why is this?

The factory system was, and remains, crucial for the purposes of profitable production for a number of reasons. Most importantly, it enables owners to exercise close control over workers to ensure they work efficiently and conscientiously (Dobb, 1963). This had been extremely difficult under the earlier putting-out system in which merchants delivered raw materials to household producers and later collected the finished or partly finished items. Merchants found that production was variable and depended on the fluctuating wants and inclinations of producers. As a result, they were unable to exercise sufficient control over the producers' level of output. It was moreover difficult for them to prevent producers from using raw materials for their own purposes – a problem which was overcome by organising work in factories. Indeed, the drive towards the factory system was generally for these organisational rather than technological reasons. This is confirmed by the fact that, although in the woollen industry the spinning jenny was used in *both* the putting-out system and the early factories, the latter method of production supplanted the former. Similarly, although the technology common to both the putting-out and factory systems of the woollen industry was the handloom, the factory system had become dominant by 1800.

It would seem, then, that the advantages of inventions like the spinning jenny could only be fully utilised within the organisational context of the factory (Marglin, 1980). At the same time, the factory system enabled employers to develop and take full advantage of the enhanced efficiency and control which became possible when production was sub-divided into specialised and interdependent tasks. As early as 1776, Adam Smith had pointed out that this 'technical division of labour' made work more productive. This was because employees would be more diligent in exercising specific tasks, while at the same time the productive process as a whole could be more tightly controlled (Smith, 1910).

It was only when the factory system was proven to be a more profitable and efficient form of production that it acted as a spur to technical innovations. The various forms that technological change took were shaped by the requirements of the factories; primarily, the need to improve the quality and quantity of goods for sale in the market. At the same time, they provided contexts within which the patents and licences associated with technical inventions could be protected (Marglin, 1980). Indeed, the early factories, consisting of workers, a division of labour and standard job routines, prepared the way for the introduction of machinery which, in the first instance, assisted labour – by making it more productive – but at a later stage replaced it. In fact, from its very beginning, the factory system encouraged the sub-division of work into increasingly simple tasks which could later be taken over by machines. None of this would have happened without the development of markets and the need for profits.

However, if the early factories were to operate more efficiently than previous productive systems, they had to impose industrial discipline (Landes, 1969). Essentially, factories were disciplinary systems since control over work performance was exercised through supervision, by the division of labour and by mechanisation. But there were wider problems. In the face of resistance to factory employment, how did the early entrepreneurs obtain a disciplined workforce? Many early factory workers were vagrants and dispossessed farm labourers who had no other means of obtaining a necessary level of subsistence. But once the factory system had become established, and because it destroyed other forms of production with its superior efficiency, other reserves of labour became available. Even so, it was necessary to introduce a system of discipline through methods of time-keeping, diligence and coercion (Thompson, 1982). If obtaining worker compliance was one of the major problems which confronted the early industrial capitalists, it was the inbuilt social controls of mechanisation which provided one of the most effective solutions.[3]

While the factory system fundamentally restructured the nature of work, its wider implications were no less great. Ultimately, it led to large-scale urbanisation through the concentration of labour within specific geographical localities. Obviously, towns had previously existed as centres of commerce, administration and culture, but now the rapidly expanding industrial labour force was to transform them out of all recognition. This urban proletariat was solely dependent upon the sale of its labour for acquiring a necessary means of subsistence and was in sharp contrast to the condition of independent artisans, craftsmen, traders and agricultural workers who were engaged in the household productive system (Engels, 1958). The latter usually possessed, or had access to, material resources whereby – even at a very minimal level – they could meet their own needs.

In the most general terms, then, production for profit, the factory system and urbanisation were the essential characteristics of the newly emerging industrial capitalist societies of the eighteenth and nineteenth centuries. Britain was in the lead, with France and Germany some way behind until the latter part of the nineteenth century. It is important not to over-emphasise the uniformity of this process as it occurred in different regions of the same country, or as it developed within different countries (Kumar, 1978). In the control of labour, for example, practices varied widely. Some employers cultivated a paternalistic strategy (Newby, 1977) – witness, for example, the strategy of many Quaker-owned family firms in the north of England – while others used a system of sub-contracting to obtain a maximum level of output with a minimum degree of personal supervision (Littler, 1980). In coal-mining in Britain, the early proprietors abdicated many employer responsibilities and avoided the problems of industrial discipline by negotiating with gang masters an agreed level of output for a particular wage price. Indeed, this system persisted in many British coal fields until they became state-owned in the 1940s, and it still continues in large sectors of the building and construction industry (Scase and Goffee, 1982).

Further, if we compare countries, it is evident that the paths of early industrialisation were far from similar. In the United States, the opening up of the western frontier created an ever-expanding market within which free and independent manufacturers could compete. In many European countries, by contrast, the persistence of feudal social structures was important. The pattern of industrialisation in Germany was heavily influenced by the Prussian aristocracy who, through the development of a highly profitable agriculture, financed the early factories. In other countries, it was either the state, as in France, or colonialism, as in Holland, Belgium and Britain, which shaped the direction and pattern of industrialisation (Bendix, 1956).

However, despite variations within and between countries, the development of industrial capitalism did produce a number of key features of the sort we have outlined – the production of commodities for profit, the creation of markets within which these were sold, the emergence of the factory system, urbanisation and the creation of an industrial labour force. But most importantly it was the factory system which became the core around which industrial society was organised. It was this fundamental change which preoccupied the early sociological thinkers.

For Durkheim, the most important consequence of the factory system was its destruction of traditional forms of social order (Durkheim, 1964). For him, industrialisation changed the nature of social solidarity. He argued that in small-scale non-industrial societies individuals are so absorbed into undifferentiated social systems that there is virtually no scope for the development of strictly personal attributes and skills. There may be divisions on the basis of age or gender which are reflected in the functional allocation of work tasks but, on the whole, most members of small-scale societies are characterised by overwhelming similarities, in terms of both their social roles and their identities. They are, then, firmly integrated within social structures in a mechanical manner. With industrialisation, however, there is an increase in the division of labour and of exchange relationships. *Mechanical* forms of social solidarity evolve into *organic* forms. Solidarity established upon similarities is replaced by that based on functional interdependences. Social cohesion is then rooted in specialised occupational roles which, in turn, foster individual differences. In Durkheim's analysis, industrialisation does not lead to the breakdown of social solidarity; instead, one form is superseded by another. Nevertheless, he felt that there were endemic strains within organic forms such that social order was always problematic.

One of the most serious of these problems for Durkheim was that the division of labour could develop pathological forms through over-specialisation.⁴ This could make it more difficult to coordinate tasks and may isolate workers to such an extent that they no longer have a sense of the whole production process. Thus, the problem of creating unity, of regulating the complexity of an organically based society, is a moral one. As a result, Durkheim developed a preoccupation with the problems of moral as well as of social integration: how can organic societies be more fully integrated? One of his solutions was to advocate professional associations which, organised around occupations, would mediate between the individual and society. Whether he had in mind forms of industrial syndicalism based upon a system of employee self-management or the development of employer-based, company guilds is uncertain.

Certainly Durkheim gives little recognition to the possibility of anything but a moral solution to the conflicts that exist between different groups in society; for example, those between employers and employees or owners and non-owners. There is, in his proposals for reform, such an emphasis upon moral regulation that fundamentally unequal relationships of domination and control are almost entirely neglected. Indeed, Durkheim places only secondary importance on the essentially capitalist nature of the industrialisation process. For him, the antagonistic relationships generated by industrialisation are not a function of property ownership or the organisation of production *per se*, but are a pathological consequence of its immature phase. Accordingly, many of his ideas have shaped a tradition in social science which, in a preoccupation with industrial problems, searches for an ultimate harmony of interests.[5] Thus many social scientists overstate the extent to which employers and employees share common interests and neglect their many conflicting objectives within a capitalist-owned productive process.[6] Although Durkheim posed important questions about social order, he gave insufficient attention to the structural sources of conflict. Indeed, it could be that his ideas will have greater relevance in some future society in which the antagonistic features of economic production may be destroyed. In a 'pure form' of socialist society in which goods are produced according to need rather than for profit, it may be possible to counter the destructiveness of abnormal forms of the division of labour, and create a harmonious social morality of the kind that Durkheim desired.[7]

Weber, in a similar manner to Durkheim, was interested in the dynamics of large-scale social change (Weber, 1964). Again, like Durkheim, he felt these could only be understood by using the historical and comparative method. Why, he asked, did capitalism develop under some historical circumstances rather than others (Weber, 1930)? The initial impetus, he argued, came from Calvinism which, through its doctrine of predestination, produced among its adherents feelings of self-doubt about their status as members of 'the elect'. In strong contrast to pre-Reformation religion, this was expressed in a this-wordly commitment to an ascetic way of life and a belief in work as a calling. For Calvinist entrepreneurs, this meant that profits should not be consumed in a conspicuous manner. On the contrary, there was the sustained pursuit of self-discipline and efficiency as virtues in themselves which, as a result, led to the development of calculative, rational work practices and to the accumulation of capital.

The major expression of this calculative rationality was the capitalist enterprise, since it embodied a number of features which were necessary for making profts in the most efficient manner. Eventually, the 'spirit of capitalism' became self-sustaining and was transformed into increasingly secular terms. For Weber, capitalism required the bureaucratic form of administration within which there was clear delineation of tasks according to fixed rules and procedures; the recruitment of officials on the basis of technical expertise; the exercise of rational-based authority; and interpersonal relations guided by impersonal and calculative criteria (Weber, 1948). Within the bureaucratic system, sentiment and personal obligations were subordinated to the rational pursuit of profit.

In addition to these features – inherent in any bureaucratic form of administration – Weber argued that the capitalist enterprise required the existence of formally free labour – which is not tied by law or tradition to any particular place of work or employer – and propertyless workers whose labour could be costed and organised in a similar calculative and rational manner as any other productive resource. Further, it needed centralised forms of control so that specialised work tasks could be systematically coordinated. So the capitalist enterprise required a hierarchy of managers and supervisors who, through the exercise of rational forms of control, could obtain the maximum output and efficiency of workers.[8] Indeed, Weber regarded the capitalist enterprise as essentially a hierarchical system of domination and control (Weber, 1964). It was, in other words, a structure of power relationships of a kind that Durkheim under-emphasised because of his preoccupation with social cohesion and moral order. But, like Durkheim, Weber argued that there was no conflict of interests between groups. The hierarchical nature of power relationships within the enterprise was necessary for the rational pursuit of profit. This functioned to integrate the activities of individuals who, despite their various positions of superordination, shared the common goal of economic self-interest. Hence, Weber's analysis of power relationships within the capitalist enterprise leads him to under-state the inherent conflict of interests between owners and non-owners.

Weber does, however, recognise the importance of the distinction between owners and non-owners. This is clear from his discussion of social class. In his view, social classes originate in the ownership and non-ownership of productive resources; in other words, the extent to which individuals have control over resources for the purposes of economic self-gain (Weber, 1964). Consequently, Weber distinguishes between *owners* who exploit various forms of property and *non-owners* who can market a variety of skills. However, Weber devotes little attention to the structure of class relations within the economic enterprise. For him, social classes are aggregates of individuals pursuing their own economic self-interests within the broad categories determined by ownership and non-ownership. The market is the universal arbiter for each social class and he sees class conflict as a fight for access to the market and for the determination of the price of products, including labour. Therefore, he is not disposed to consider the idea that 'the market' may actually conceal a much more fundamental antagonism; that is, an exploitative relationship between owners and non-owners. It is here that Marx's analysis is pertinent since he does recognise that the factory system, in producing goods to sell in the market for profit, generates irreconcilable conflicts between owners and non-owners which, in turn, lead to the formation of social classes (Marx and Engels, 1969).

Marx was interested in large-scale social change and in determining the laws of historical development. In common with Durkheim and Weber, he used a historical and comparative method which focused upon the material foundations of human societies (Marx, 1964). He gave particular priority to the mode of production – that is, to the processes whereby human societies meet their material needs. According to Marx, history may be categorised into epochs, each of which is characterised by one predominant mode of production (Marx and Engels, 1970). This, in turn, shapes the institutions, cultures, laws, religions, ideologies and the general social form of each historical epoch. He argued that it was possible to identify various modes of production as they had existed in human history: the asiatic, the feudal and the capitalist.

In the asiatic mode of production – which Marx believed existed in ancient India, Mexico and Peru – there is virtually no economic surplus (which is to say that goods are not produced in excess of the immediate material requirements of the producers). In such societies there is only a rudimentary division of work tasks and, because of the absence of an economic surplus, there is little distinction between producers and non-producers. Accordingly, there is no extraction – or expropriation – of the economic product by non-producers. Hence, within the context of self-sustaining rural communities and in the absence of private property ownership, there is no material basis for the formation of antagonistic social groupings – that is, social classes. Instead, any economic surplus is held and consumed in common. However, with the development of the division of labour and progress in the technical tools of production, it is possible for there to be the production of an economic surplus. As this occurs, a new mode of production becomes dominant within which groups of non-producers expropriate the economic surplus created by others. This expropriated economic surplus then becomes the private property of the non-producers. Thus, within the feudal mode of production, the nobility expropriated the surplus created by the peasantry while under capitalism, the bourgeoisie expropriate the economic surplus produced by the proletariat (Marx and Engels, 1969).

Each historical mode of production is therefore characterised by productive relationships that are essentially exploitative; between, on the one hand, the producers of the economic surplus and, on the other, the non-producers who own the means of production. In each mode of production, the producers create the economic surplus which becomes the personal wealth and property of the non-producers (Marx and Engels, 1969). This relationship constitutes the structural basis for conflict and struggle between the two classes. Such class struggles are the underlying forces of social change because the irreconcilable nature of the antagonism can only lead to the destruction of the existing mode of production. Hence, for Marx, all history is the history of class struggles and all such struggles are the locomotive of historical change. Each mode of production, therefore, contains the seeds of its own destruction: the formation of capitalism, for instance, created a class of propertyless producers – the proletariat – which then, according to Marx, poses a threat to its own existence. For him, it was only with the abolition of capitalism, the transition to socialism and eventually to communism, that production ceases to be organised on a selfdestructive basis. Only in communism are there no classes, and since these are the forces of social change, history ends (Marx and Engels, 1969). Marx's theory of capitalism and socialism, therefore, hinges on his understanding of classes and class conflict. It is useful to summarise his theory of class in a more explicit manner.

The basis for the formation of classes is the social relations of production; more specifically, the arrangements for the production and expropriation of the economic surplus. This is then reflected in the ownership and non-ownership of property, including, of course, the technical means of production. As a result, within a mode of production, there can only be two basic classes, consisting of those who produce and those who expropriate the economic surplus. Classes confront each other within a mutually hostile relationship, but they are also mutually interdependent; it follows, therefore, that a class can only exist on the basis of expropriation if there is another class producing the economic surplus. Nevertheless, the relationship between them is inherently unstable and, as a result, it is necessary for the expropriator class – for instance, the nobility under feudalism and the bourgeoisie under capitalism – to justify or legitimate its own exploitative position. Hence, the need for various political and cultural institutions which correspond to the needs of the 'material base' of society (Marx and Engels, 1970). In fact, Marx believed these institutions to be a 'superstructure' which is linked to the 'base' (Marx, 1975). But, to the extent that this process of legitimation is successful, it conceals class antagonisms.

Within capitalism, Marx therefore differentiates between a *class in itself* and a *class for itself*; a class in itself is a force of struggle only when its members have developed a sufficient level of collective awareness to be a class for itself (Marx and Engels, 1969). In practice, there are considerable barriers to the formation of class consciousness because of the effectiveness of ideological institutions which, for example through their appeal to the values of individualism, negate class awareness and serve to maintain the position of the capitalist class. But it is always possible to refer to a class in itself since classes exist by virtue of the antagonistic nature of the social relations of production and not by virtue of the attitudes and beliefs to which members of a class may subscribe. Indeed, as we shall argue in a later chapter, the antagonistic relationship between wage labour and capital is provoking a 'crisis' within the productive process even without the development of a broadly based class consciousness.[9] In other words, the breakdown of the capitalist mode of production does not necessarily require open and conscious class struggle. The transition from feudalism to capitalism has sometimes taken place without revolutionary struggle (Marx, 1974); so, too, may the transition from capitalism to socialism.

Marx, then, constructed a theory of social change which gave primacy to the antagonistic nature of production relations. It is within the processes by which the material needs of society are met that the forces of social change are located. Within this perspective, Marx devoted special attention to the development of the capitalist mode of production as it had taken shape in England. It was historically the most mature example and he distinguished four stages in its development. These were pre-capitalist *simple commodity production* and, within the capitalist mode of production, the stages of *cooperation, manufacture* and *modern industry* (Marx, 1974).

According to Marx, the process 'that clears the way for the capitalist system, can be none other than the process which takes away from the labourer the possession of his means of production, a process that transforms, on the one hand, the social means of subsistence and of production into capital, on the other, the immediate producers into wage labourers' (Marx, 1974). This, for Marx, had its beginnings in the sixteenth century in Britain and was brought about by land enclosure which created landless agricultural workers. Their labour became their sole means of subsistence because they lost their traditional means of production. At the same time, wealth became concentrated in the hands of landlords and merchants. Unfortunately, Marx devotes little attention to the way in which this wealth was used for the accumulation of *capital*; in other words, how it was used for productive purposes, for producing commodities for sale in the market. However, he recognises that during this transitional period, merchant capital was transferred into various rural-based industries, especially spinning and weaving, such that small-scale commodity production was increasingly subject to the dictates of merchants.

Simple commodity production was still pre-capitalist because producers were essentially artisans or craft workers who performed all-round skills. It was an independent form of production in which there was little or no division of labour; any rudimentary breakdown of tasks was between men and women, adults and children, within the family system. Accordingly, there was an absence of wage labour and little distinction between work and other domestic activities. The family was, essentially, the unit of economic production. Further, the producers owned simple hand-implements and tools which were an extension of their own craft skills. Unlike present-day factory operatives, they owned their tools of production and, under the conditions of simple commodity production, they enjoyed considerable autonomy in the performance of their work tasks. Even so, there were significant constraints: they had to produce commodities of a type and quality that were acceptable to merchants, traders and other customers; at the same time, they had to work to a sufficient level of intensity in order to produce and sell enough to provide a level of subsistence for themselves and their families. But within these constraints, they could determine the pace and the frequency of their own work.

However, during the sixteenth and seventeenth centuries in Britain, the trading and work situation of craft workers changed. This was primarily because merchants were extending their control over the process of commodity production. Increasingly, they stipulated the conditions of production, so the producers lost much of their traditional autonomy. Hence, the 'putting-out' system gradually developed in which the merchants delivered the raw materials, extended credit and later collected the completed commodities. Merchants paid for these after deducting the cost of raw materials. As a result, producers gradually became dependent upon the merchants for the supply of raw materials, for work and, hence, for their livelihood. Because of competition between producers, the merchants were able to determine the price, quality and quantity of products.

This is the juncture at which the capitalist mode of production *proper* originates; merchants became capitalists. The details are uncertain but it was marked by the destruction of the putting-out system and its replacement by factories. *Cooperation*, the first stage of capitalism, was characterised by the concentration of producers in small workshops, under direct supervision (Marx, 1974). But the producers continued to work in ways which resembled the domestic system. These early workshops, in other words, were little more than assemblages of producers who exercised many of their traditional skills. Nevertheless, the shift of production from the household to the early workshops constituted, for Marx, a fundamental change in the productive process. As he states:

Capitalist production only then really begins... when each individual capital employs simultaneously a comparatively large number of labourers; when, consequently, the labour process is carried out on an extensive scale and yields, relatively, large quantities of products. A greater number of labourers working together, at the same time, in one place... in order to produce the same sort of commodity under the mastership of one capitalist, constitutes, both historically and logically, the starting-point of capitalist production. (Marx, 1974, p. 305)

However, he acknowledges that there is little difference between the early workshops and previous forms of production in terms of technique. He claims that the new mode of production 'is hardly to be distinguished in its earliest stages, from the handicraft trades of the guilds, otherwise than by the greater number of workmen simultaneously employed by one and the same individual capital. The workshop of the medieval master craftsman is simply enlarged' (Marx, 1974, p. 305).

However, this period of simple cooperation is rapidly superseded by that of *manufacture*, as the early capitalists endeavoured to take full advantage of the factory system. This stage was important for the development of the division of labour since it deprived producers of many of their traditional, all-round skills. They no longer produced complete, finished commodities; indeed, they became, to use Marx's term, *detail* workers capable of performing only a limited number of tasks within a complex and interdependent division of labour. As a result, the production of commodities becomes a social rather than an individual process, demanding the concomitant specialised skills of a number of producers. Further, these producers no longer own the technical means of production; instead, capitalists own the machines and the operative's hand-tools as well as the factories. Thus the producers' *sole* contribution to the work process is their labour power. This is sold to capitalists in return for a wage which is then spent on subsistence needs. In other words, producers become wage labourers who are alienated both from the means of production and from the product of their labour. Capitalists, on the other hand, own both the means of production and the product of wage labour. They pay wages so that workers may live at a socially defined level of subsistence. But for this outlay they expect a return in the production of goods with an exchange value greater than the value of the money they have spent on wages and the other costs of production. This surplus value is then used either for the capitalists' own personal consumption or for reinvestment in the productive process – in other words, to build new and larger factories which will generate yet more profit. During this stage of manufacture, capitalists personally perform most of the functions of supervision and control to ensure that they can obtain maximum production from their workers for a minimum cost.

For Marx, the nature of the capitalist mode of production is changed by the widespread introduction of machinery. He called this the stage of *modern industry* (Marx, 1974). In Britain, its origins are in the eighteenth century and are normally referred to as the industrial revolution. During this stage, there is the creation of productive systems as highly integrated mechanical *and* social processes. This brings about a further extension of the detailed division of labour such that work tasks are highly fragmented into simple and highly repetitive operations. If, under the conditions of manufacture, producers still *use* tools for the performance of tasks, within the stage of modern industry they become appendages to machines. If in manufacture there is a hierarchy of skills, in modern industry mechanisation produces homogeneous workforces of machine-minders. While in manufacture, the production of commodities is a group activity within which there is the exercise of different craft skills, in the modern factory tasks are broken down into a technical/machine-based division of labour. Consequently, the performance of work is deprived of meaning for workers since they cease to exercise any fundamental control over their own activities. Instead, mechanisation dictates the sequence and pace of work tasks and, as such, enables capitalists to extend their control over producers. In other words, the subordination of labour to capital is significantly enhanced. If under manufacture, workers were able to exercise some, albeit limited, control over the performance of their work tasks, they were, nevertheless, by virtue of their dependence upon the sale of their labour, *formally* subordinated to capitalists. But with modern industry, workers are part and parcel of a collective labour process in which their activities are precisely defined within a detailed division of labour. Thus, by comparison with craft workers in the stage of manufacture, producers in modern industry retain few skills that can be exercised independently of the capitalist-owned productive process. In other words, there is the *real* subordination of labour to capital.[10]

With an increase in the scale of production, Marx saw that it was necessary for capitalists to delegate many of their functions. Consequently, supervision and control become increasingly allocated to managers while ownership ceases to be the sole preserve of individual proprietors or partnerships. Since the growth in size of the capitalist enterprise in England during the nineteenth century required larger amounts of capital, there was the emergence of a new legal, corporate entity, the limited liability joint-stock company. With the advent of shareholders, ownership – like control – becomes a collective rather than solely an individual responsibility.

These, briefly, are the stages in the development of the capitalist mode of production as identified by Marx. Of course, we have merely outlined, as simply as possible, a detailed and complex process. Although his account of development in England ends in the middle of the nineteenth century, Marxist writers have extended his analysis to describe further changes in the capitalist mode of production which have occurred during the late nineteenth and twentieth centuries. Some of these writers have identified a fourth stage – that of monopoly capital – within which the forces developing within Marx's stage of modern industry have become more fully expressed (Baran and Sweezy, 1966; Braverman, 1974; Friedman, 1977). They argue that although a range of complex technical and scientific occupations has been created, the continuing development of capitalist-sponsored technology has further deskilled large sectors of the labour force. At the same time, through a process of mergers and amalgamations, there has been the growth of large-scale national and multinational corporations. Furthermore, instead of these being subject to what Marx considered to be the anarchy of the market, they have reached such a level of monopolisation that they can now largely dictate the nature of market forces. In fact, according to many Marxists, the stage of monopoly capital vividly expresses the inherent contradictions of this particular mode of production; the expansion of capitalist corporations has brought about the internationalisation of both production and markets, the over-supply of commodities and, thus, a tendency for profit rates to fall (Mandel, 1975).

In this chapter we have tried to outline the essential characteristics of the emerging capitalist industrial system as it appeared to Durkheim, Weber and Marx. It is now necessary to direct our attention to the core features of present-day capitalism. This, in turn, will lead us to a detailed analysis of social class and stratification as these affect life styles and life chances in contemporary Western countries.

2

Capitalism, Class and Inequality

In the analysis of capitalism, it is possible to do two things: first, to identify the core features of the mode of production, and secondly, to describe their *expression* within different countries. The analysis of capitalism is often undertaken with the assumption that the features described for any one country can be generalised to others.[1] Alternatively, the nature of modern capitalism is discussed at such a level of abstraction that little importance is attached to differences between countries.[2] We feel, however, that the distinction between the core features of the capitalist mode of production and their expression in different countries is important. For instance, although the internationalisation of capital has occurred in the twentieth century – both in terms of productive processes and in the scale of markets – capitalist production is still situated within national boundaries, and this has fundamental implications for the dynamics of capitalism as a mode of production. For instance, miners in South Africa, the United States and France may all be regarded as *similar* wage labourers. But a study of their living and working conditions, of their social, political and legal rights, would instantly disclose fundamental *differences* between them. Equally, the *expression* of class relationships in terms of life styles, attitudes and beliefs often varies from one country to the next. Thus, before discussing some of these variations in the next chapter, we will examine the core features of the capitalist mode of production.

The essential feature of capitalism is the production of goods and services for profit.[3] This profit is then used for further production in order to obtain further profits. Capitalism, then, is a process of accumulation. Capitalists – whether they are individual proprietors of small-scale enterprises or large joint-stock companies with institutional shareholders – start off with quantities of money for investment (M). With this money, the capitalist can purchase a factory, machinery, energy, materials and labour – in other words, establish a productive process for the purpose of producing commodities (C). These commodities are then sold in the market for a price such that, after the costs incurred in their production and sale have been taken into account, the capitalist makes a profit (M_1). This profit can then either be consumed in the form of dividends and distributed profits or be reinvested in the productive process in order to extend production and make further profits (M_2). In other words, whether it be in South Africa or Sweden, the principle underlying the capitalist mode of production is the same and may be expressed as follows:

$$M \rightarrow C \rightarrow M_1 \rightarrow C \rightarrow M_2 \rightarrow$$

This is the central imperative of the capitalist mode of production. Even the most socially committed and altruistically minded entrepreneur or capitalist enterprise must respect this law; if not, bankruptcy threatens!

The capitalist productive process is characterised by the creation of two types of value. First, as raw materials are converted into commodities, they become useful. Raw materials, in themselves, are valueless; it is only when they are worked upon that they acquire *use values*. Trees standing in a forest may be aesthetically pleasing but they only become useful when labour is expended upon them; when they have been cut down and converted into such items as furniture, buildings or even logs for heating. Use value, then, is always a function of the labour expended upon converting raw materials into usable commodities. This value-creating function of labour is a feature of all modes of production.

Second, what gives this process a specifically capitalist character is that the value added by the producers which is embodied in the market value or *exchange value* of the commodity is not entirely distributed to the producers in the form of wages. Rather it is expropriated by capitalist owners and becomes their own private property. To put the matter simply but crudely, the owners *profit* from the labour of others. Conversely, the producers never receive the total value of the commodities which they create. If they did, there would be no profits and the capitalist enterprise would ultimately become bankrupt. Profits, then, are a function of the expropriation of the economic surplus from producers who must, by definition, be exploited, despite the emotive connotations of the word. *Exploitation*, is an inherent feature of the capitalist mode of production. But not all labour tasks directly contribute to the creation of profits, although they are often needed for this purpose. Caretakers and security officers, for example, are 'unproductive' and yet they are usually necessary; private premises and factories, for instance, need to be protected.

While some of the economic surplus which capitalist owners acquire is normally consumed in the form of distributed profits, the rest is reinvested in the productive process, for two major reasons. First, to replace depleted stock and to renovate the forces of production. Second, in order to remain competitive. The enterprise has to modernise continuously and rationalise the productive process through modernisation and technological development if it is to remain efficient. It is only in these ways that productivity can be increased, since there is a limit to the length of the working day and to the intensity at which employees can work. Mechanisation, in other words, enables capitalist owners to increase the economic surplus which they can derive from the labour of their producers.

If capitalism is characterised by the production of commodities for sale in the market at a profit, it is also distinguished from other modes of production by the existence of *free* labour. This is a feature that was stressed by both Marx and Weber. Workers are free to sell their labour in exchange for wages. This labour is a commodity and therefore, like all commodities, is bought and sold in the market. The worker sells the capacity to produce commodities in order to obtain a wage. Conversely, capitalists will only buy this labour so long as it creates value and thereby profits. But labour is also free under capitalism in the sense that it is 'unfettered'. By comparison with the ties which bound the peasant under feudalism, the worker is unattached.[4] Consequently, the free-wage labourer can only obtain the means of subsistence through the 'cash nexus'; that is, through the sale of labour to the capitalist in the market place. Once purchased, this capacity to labour is 'owned' by the capitalist.

These are some of the key features of the capitalist mode of production. But they only constitute a skeleton. It is necessary to elaborate upon this in order to produce a more satisfactory and complete picture. We shall concentrate upon present-day features and, in this sense, our analysis will refer to the stage of monopoly capitalism. Accordingly, we shall take account of such features as the institutional ownership of capitalist corporations, state intervention, the sub-division of the old-style capitalists' functions into various 'managerial' and 'professional' occupations, and the nature of present-day stratification systems. As a result, this broader picture of capitalist society may be summarised as figure 1.

The 'core' of the capitalist mode of production is represented in the top left-hand corner of the figure with the process of accumulation indicated by the heavily printed arrows. As we have stated, not all of the economic surplus is reinvested; some of it is distributed to shareholders as dividends while a further proportion is taken by the state in taxes. These taxes, in turn, are often used to provide the various services which, directly and indirectly, meet some of the needs of the capitalist accumulation process. Companies need, for example, to operate within contexts of relative socio-political stability. Further, they normally require healthy and literate workforces. So the state in Western capitalist countries requires revenue in order to meet these needs. The productive process itself, however, consists of two major aspects: the technical means and the social relations of production. We shall now discuss each of these in turn.

It is self-evident that the modern capitalist productive process requires factories, machinery, raw materials and the use of non-human sources of energy such as electricity. It is less evident why labour should be regarded as a means of production in the same manner as machinery. The reason is quite simple: it is costed by the capitalist enterprise in the same way as any other factor of production. Labour is the exercise of energy which, like machinery, is used to convert raw materials and components into commodities. As Marx argued, machinery is nothing more than the substitution of 'dead labour' (machinery) for 'living labour' (Marx, 1974). As we have stated earlier, competition between capitalist enterprises fuels the quest for greater productivity through technological innovation and the use, as far as possible, of 'cheap' labour. A production system consisting of semi- and unskilled workers on the

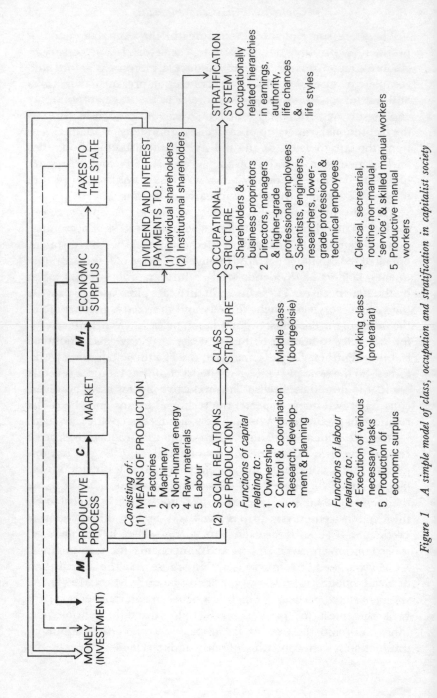

Figure 1 A simple model of class, occupation and stratification in capitalist society

assembly-line can produce a greater volume of standardised commodities for the market at a cheaper cost than a more 'traditional' labour-intensive process dependent upon skilled craftsmen (Braverman, 1974).

However, the productive process does not consist simply of technical means or factors. It is also a structure of social relationships within which the different functions of capital accumulation are undertaken. These are, in turn: (1) ownership; (2) control and coordination; (3) research, development and planning; (4) the execution of other necessary tasks; and (5) the production of the economic surplus. The first three may be referred to as functions of capital, the remainder as functions of labour. Ownership stipulates the goals and means whereby the functions of capital are to be attained. Historically, the capitalist ownership function has been expressed in a variety of forms, from the entrepreneur or owner-manager to the shareholders of large-scale, joint-stock companies (Scott, 1979). These shareholders may consist of numerous individual or private investors or, perhaps, a very limited number of representatives of banks, pension funds, investment trusts and other financial institutions. Similarly, the ownership function may be closely integrated with managerial control, as with the old-style entrepreneur (Bendix, 1956). Alternatively, there may be a significant degree of separation between them, as is the case in many present-day corporations (Scott, 1979). But whatever the nature of the ownership function, the logic of the capitalist mode of production demands that the overriding goal of the business enterprise is profit.

This relentless pursuit of profit requires the exercise of the functions of coordination and control. Any system of production with a division of labour, whether capitalist or not, requires coordination; in other words, it is necessary for tasks to be integrated within a work process. But the capitalist-owned corporation also requires the exercise of control to ensure that the work process operates at a sufficient level of economic efficiency to create profits for the owners. Marx predicted that, with the abolition of the capitalist mode of production and its inherent quest for profit, there would be little need for a distinctive control function. Although coordination would still be required, the function of control would become redundant (Marx and Engels, 1969).

During the stages of capitalism which Marx described as those of cooperation and manufacture, the functions of ownership and control were personally undertaken by the capitalist or entrepreneur (Marx, 1974). It is with the later stages of modern industry and monopoly capitalism that the function of control becomes separated from ownership, creating various managerial and supervisory positions. The growth in size of capitalist corporations has complicated the tasks of control and coordination, demanding ever-increasing numbers of managers and other specialist supervisors. This process is inherent in the development of the capitalist mode of production and, accordingly, rebuts the claim that the proliferation of managers and other administrative employees unattached to the ownership function heralds a 'post-capitalist' society (Bell, 1973). Even if there is some separation between the functions of ownership and control, the task of managers is delegated from the ownership function and they must, in the final analysis, be associated with the owners' quest for profit and long-term capital accumulation.

With the growth of management, the increasing technical complexity of the productive process requires continuous research, development and planning. It is no longer possible for the modern corporation, in the manner of its nineteenth-century predecessor, to be purely responsive to erratic and fluctuating consumer preferences. Instead, the modern corporation has to conduct detailed and systematic research into new products, determine their potential profitability, continually reorganise the work process, retrain workers, invest in new machinery and equipment, and consciously create a demand for the product through intensive marketing, advertising and sales campaigns. The costs can be enormous; the launch of a new motor vehicle, for example, can be at least £500 million. In other words, the exploration of new avenues of profitability by capitalist corporations requires large numbers of scientists, engineers, market researchers, designers, cost accountants and other specialists. This accounts for the rapid expansion of these occupations during the twentieth century. But not all of these tasks are related to corporate expansion and diversification. Many have been directed towards intensifying the work process and to raising productivity in the pursuit of profit. The occupations of work-study engineers, systems analysts, industrial psychologists and operations researchers may be interpreted in these terms.[5]

So far, we have devoted attention to the functions of capital. But there are, of course, the activities associated with the functions of labour. There are those that may be regarded as unproductive but necessary, while there are others that directly contribute to the production of profits or the economic surplus. Among the former are those functions performed by routine, lower-grade administrative and technical workers. These activities are unproductive in the sense that they do not directly produce an economic surplus but they are necessary for the performance of other productive tasks. The functions of ownership, control and coordination, and development and planning all require back-up. Thus, for example, scientists and technologists require assistants and laboratory technicians; market researchers need computer programmers and survey analysts; and managers and other supervisors need secretarial, clerical and lower-grade administrative assistance. The rapid growth of these positions during the twentieth century constitutes an integral process within the development of the capitalist corporation. In this sense, they cannot be regarded as the legacy of the clerks of the small-scale enterprises of the nineteenth century. These were concerned with the tasks of control and coordination which are now undertaken by managers and other high-level administrative staff.

Finally, there are those functions which are directly related to the production of the economic surplus. Within a capitalist-owned manufacturing enterprise, the production of the economic surplus is dependent upon the conversion of raw materials and previously created components into commodities for sale in the market.[6] It is this function which creates the economic surplus since those who perform this task do not receive as wages the total amount of the value of the commodities which they produce. All the other tasks within the capitalist enterprise, then, are dependent upon this value-creating function because, without the exploitation of productive work, there can be no economic surplus. Clearly, the nature of productive work has changed considerably with developments in the capitalist mode of production. During the present stage of monopoly capital, for instance, there has been a contraction of skill differentials, a polarisation of labour markets and an increasing routinisation of work tasks. The general deskilling of both non-productive and productive work has had fundamental implications for the nature of occupational experiences, life styles and attitudes (Braverman, 1974).[7]

The productive process, then, requires the performance of a number of functions: those of ownership; control and coordination; development and planning; the execution of unproductive but necessary tasks; and the production of the economic surplus. Although the manner in which these functions are fulfilled may vary considerably – producing a variety of organisational forms associated with size, technical complexity, the commodities produced and market conditions – no capitalist corporation is able to exist without the effective performance of them. The functions of control and coordination, for instance, are always necessary, although they may be undertaken by the 'old-style' entrepreneur or, as in large enterprises, by managers and professionals within complex bureaucratic administrative structures.

It is within the social relations of production that we can locate the origins of class. In line with Marx's claim that social classes are rooted in the production and expropriation of the economic surplus, it is possible to allocate the various functions within the productive process to the two major classes: the bourgeoisie and proletariat. Class, therefore, has an objective basis – the social relations of production – which exists quite independently of the consciousness of those who undertake the various functions (Marx and Engels, 1969). In terms of the functions performed within the capitalist enterprise, those associated with capital – that is, ownership, control and coordination, development and planning – constitute the structural basis for the bourgeoisie or middle class; those functions relating to labour – that is, the production of the economic surplus – are essentially proletarian or working class.

But what of those functions pertaining to the execution of unproductive but necessary tasks? Since they do not directly contribute to the economic surplus they are not obviously working class in their nature. But, at the same time, they are not directly related to the capitalist functions of ownership and control such that they may be viewed as middle class. So the objective class position of those undertaking these tasks is, on the face of it, ambiguous. However, in view of the fact that these tasks are typically routine, narrowly prescribed and subject to the authority and commands of others, they may be regarded, albeit in a marginal sense, as working class. In other words, and notwithstanding the fact that the earnings of those undertaking these functions are dependent upon the economic surplus created by others, these tasks are essentially low-skilled and subject to detailed managerial scrutiny. Indeed, as discussed later in this chapter, that is reflected in the location of these occupations within the earnings-related stratification system.

The class structure, then, is derived from the social relations of production. As such, it has an objective reality. But, at the same time, it tends to be obscured or hidden in everyday life. This is because the functions of capital and labour do not express themselves as class positions but as occupational positions. It is occupations rather than class that make up the everyday reality of the productive process. They constitute the major basis for personal identity, social relationships, attitudes and behaviour. (That may of course change if work, occupations and careers become less significant in the future because of a general decline in the availability of full-time employment. In that case, personal identities may become more completely constructed according to various 'non-occupational' criteria.) One of the major factors which inhibits class consciousness – 'class for itself' as distinct from 'class in itself' – is the pattern of ideas and behaviour associated with occupational experience and identity. In short, occupational divisions are the major source of cleavages within present-day capitalist society. The occupational structure, therefore, is an expression of the social relations of production. It is, in turn, the basis for the stratification system (Parkin, 1971).

In theory, it is possible for there to be any number of stratification systems, simply because they are hierarchical orders within which individuals and groups can be ranked. It is, for example, possible to rank people according to such criteria as income, prestige, patterns of expenditure, life chances, authority and so on. However, in a capitalist society, any ranking on the basis of these criteria would quickly reveal a pattern characterised by two major features. First, all of the above-mentioned factors are closely associated with each other; a person with high earnings tends to enjoy high social prestige, above-average length of life expectancy, and so on (Reid, 1981). Secondly, in a capitalist society, the occupational structure forms the backbone of the stratification system. Thus, occupations may be ranked hierarchically in terms of income, prestige, authority,

life styles and life chances. But, of these various factors, income
is the most important since it enables individuals to obtain various
economic and social privileges. As shown in figure 1, it is possible
to rank occupational categories according to socio-economic criteria
as follows:

1 Shareholders and business proprietors.
2 Directors, managers and higher-grade professional employees.
3 Scientists, engineers, researchers, lower-grade professional and
   technical employees.
4 Clerical, secretarial, routine non-manual, 'service' and skilled
   manual workers.
5 Semi- and unskilled manual workers.

However, it is important to bear in mind that an analysis of social
stratification which uses the occupational structure as its basis is
not an alternative to the study of class relationships. It is, rather,
an approach which focuses upon the visible features of the productive
process rather than the underlying structural characteristics. Thus
income inequalities which arise from the performance of different
functions in the productive process do not express themselves in
a dichotomous or two-class manner, but in a continuous hierarchy.[8]
Although income differentials may vary over time and between
Western countries, the overall pattern has been relatively consistent
(Sawyer, 1976). If significant change has occurred in recent decades,
it has been in terms of an increasing polarisation between highly
rewarded proprietorial, managerial, professional and technical
occupations (categories 1 to 3) and the remainder, consisting of
routine non-manual and manual occupations (categories 4 and 5)
(Braverman, 1974).

A person's occupation has remained the most relevant factor in
shaping his or her social and political consciousness; it is by
reference to occupational groupings that trade unions, professional
associations and political parties organise their activities (Noble,
1981). In fact, most cleavages, tensions and struggles within the
social fabric of capitalist society express themselves in occupational
rather than in class terms. At the personal level, too, success tends
to be measured in terms of career advancement or upward mobility
within the occupational structure, leading to the acquisition of

enhanced economic and social rewards. Occupational mobility, therefore, is the most useful index of movement within and between social classes in capitalist society (Heath, 1981).

The extent to which middle-class occupations – consisting of managerial, professional and technical employees – are economically privileged can be demonstrated by reference to data for Britain, as presented in figure 2. This documents the pattern of *life-time earnings* for different occupational groups in 1980. This is a more

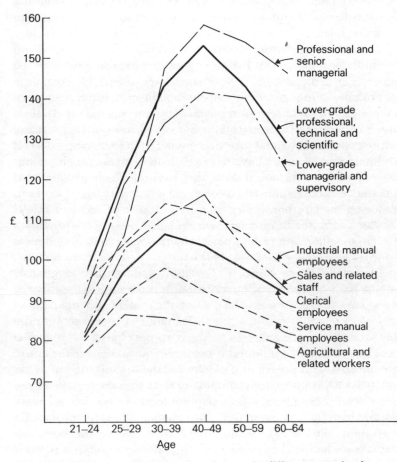

Figure 2   Median gross weekly earnings, by age, for different occupational groups in Britain, 1980 (taken from Department of Employment, 1980, table 128)

useful guide to the discontinuities that exist within the occupational structure than calculations based upon average earnings at any single point in time. This is because life-time earnings disclose the importance of the middle-class career and the incremental structure of middle-class salaries. Further, they avoid the conflation effect that occurs in calculations of occupational averages which include younger, lesser-paid managerial employees at the beginning of their careers. Obviously, this reduces the average earnings of managerial and professional groups, creating the impression of a greater degree of equality within the occupational structure than actually exists.

The increasing polarisation between managerial, professional and scientific occupations on the one hand, and the remainder on the other, is an expression of changes which have occurred in the nature of work under the stage of monopoly capitalism. It is a consequence of innovations in the technical means of production and the development of managerial control systems which have stripped many white-collar and manual jobs of their skills (Braverman, 1974). If technological changes have created a demand for engineering, scientific and technological skills, they have also further fragmented the work tasks of routine while-collar and industrial manual workers, reducing their responsibility and discretion. The ideas of F. W. Taylor and 'scientific management' embody many of the principles which, together with technological change, have contributed most to this 'deskilling' (Taylor, 1947).

Essentially, the proponents of scientific management argue that, on the basis of systematic observation, it is possible to identify the *one best way* to execute tasks. As a result, the content and organisation of jobs can be specified in a scientific manner in order to optimise the productivity of employees for the purposes of profit. It is argued that this can best be attained if management takes over the entire responsibility for the content of jobs and the organisation of work, with the effect that all decision-making capacities are removed from the worker. Management thus acquires total control over the work process through its monopoly of technical skills, planning and operational knowledge, while those responsible for the execution of tasks – whether they be routine white-collar or manual workers – no longer have the opportunity to exercise responsibility and judgement in the productive process (Braverman, 1974). In short, the application of scientific management has reinforced the *real* subordination of labour to capital (Marx, 1974).

If, under the stage of monopoly capitalism, the experience of work has become more alienating for most employees, this in turn has created further difficulties for managerial control. How does management cope with the problems associated with 'unsatisfying' work experiences such as low productivity, misuse of machinery, absenteeism, high labour turnover and industrial disputes (Salaman, 1981)? There are at least two possibilities: either to replace labour with machinery or to tighten managerial control. The application of scientific management can be considered as the most sophisticated expression of this managerial response. However, the effectiveness of this strategy has been increasingly reappraised. There have, for instance, been experiments in 'responsible autonomy' which, as an alternative, allow routine white-collar and industrial manual workers a greater degree of discretion in the performance of their tasks (Friedman, 1977). Experiments of this kind include 'job enrichment', 'job enlargement' and 'group' or 'team' production methods. Such autonomy, however, is always bound by the managerial quest for profit. Furthermore, there is a potential risk for the capitalist corporation: worker autonomy may stimulate demands for increased control which could challenge key spheres of managerial prerogative (Nichols, 1975).

Such innovations, however, have not prevented the overall polarisation of occupations within the capitalist economies. In fact, in most of these countries, there has been the formation of dual labour markets (Friedman, 1977). On the one hand, there is a *primary* labour market consisting of those occupations which are most central to the activities of capitalist corporations. These include managerial professional and technical jobs which enjoy a considerable degree of working autonomy, high pay, good conditions of employment and relatively high job security. On the other hand, there is a *secondary* labour market consisting of peripheral workers – that is, of those whose skills are seen as dispensable and which can be easily replaced by others. These tend to be semi- and unskilled manual jobs which are characterised by low pay, poor working conditions and a low level of job security. Such 'peripheral' jobs, which are most vulnerable during periods of economic recession, tend to be filled by 'reserve armies' of those who, for various reasons, do not possess the necessary qualifications, training and experience for entry into primary market, central occupations. In most capitalist countries, this reserve army consists of women, ethnic minorities, migrants, school-leavers and the pre-retired. In recent years, corporations which require a large proportion of semi- and unskilled labour have often moved their routine assembly processes to South America and south-east Africa since, in these areas, labour is even cheaper and more dispensable than in the secondary markets of Western Europe and the United States (Jordan, 1982). The effect in the older industrial countries is a higher level of unemployment among peripheral workers, which further reinforces the polarisation of occupational structures into primary and secondary sectors.

There has been a tendency for modern educational systems to respond to these trends in the labour market. Entry into primary-sector occupations is largely restricted to a small minority of those who have proceeded from the higher streams of comprehensive schools to universities and other institutions of higher education, and then into various kinds of professional and managerial training (Reid, 1981). This is the inevitable route for children from working-class backgrounds if they are to achieve occupational success. Managerial and professional workers, however, can exercise a degree of choice in assisting the careers of their children. They can either expose them to the competitive rigours of the comprehensive system or 'buy' for them private schooling so that their chances of obtaining the necessary 'meritocratic' qualifications are improved. Although many working-class children acquire higher educational qualifications and obtain various managerial and professional occupations, their chances are far less than those of their middle-class counterparts. They are much more likely to complete their education in the lower and middle streams of comprehensive schools and then, if not becoming unemployed, to enter different routine non-manual and manual occupations (Noble, 1981). Despite some inter-generational upward mobility within the class structure, therefore, the general pattern is for children to achieve similar class positions as those of their parents. Although the growth in scale of capitalist enterprises and the increasing technical complexity of productive processes have had important repercussions for career and, thus, mobility patterns, there is an overriding tendency for class recruitment to be inter-generationally *reproduced*. In Britain, for example, in a study of social mobility conducted in 1972, it was found that for men between the ages of 25 and 64 almost one-half of those who were higher-grade professional, administrative and managerial employees and large business proprietors were from homes with fathers in similar occupations (Goldthorpe, 1980). At the same time, only 7 per cent came from semi- and unskilled manual and agricultural backgrounds. Some details of this study are provided in table 1.

TABLE 1   SOCIAL ORIGINS OF THOSE IN MANAGERIAL, PROFESSIONAL AND TECHNICAL OCCUPATIONS IN BRITAIN IN 1972

Father's class	Respondent's class (%)								
	I	II	III	IV	V	VI	VII	Total	N
I	48.4	18.9	9.3	8.2	4.5	4.5	6.2	100.0	582
II	31.9	22.6	10.7	8.0	9.2	9.6	8.0	100.0	477
III	19.2	15.7	10.8	8.6	13.0	15.0	17.8	100.1	594
IV	12.8	11.1	7.8	24.9	8.7	14.7	19.9	99.9	1223
V	15.4	13.2	9.4	8.0	16.6	20.1	17.2	99.9	939
VI	8.4	8.9	8.4	7.1	12.2	29.6	25.4	100.0	2312
VII	6.9	7.8	7.9	6.8	12.5	23.5	34.8	100.2	2216
% of total number of respondents	14.3	11.4	8.6	9.9	11.6	20.8	23.3	99.9	(8343)

Occupational composition of social classes
Social class I   —   higher-grade professional (both employed and salaried), administrators, managers and large proprietors
Social class II   —   lower-grade professionals, administrators and managers, higher-grade technicians, and the supervisors of non-manual labour
Social class III —   routine clerical workers, sales personnel and other rank and file non-manual workers
Social class IV   —   farmers, small proprietors and self-employed workers
Social class V   —   supervisors of manual workers and lower-grade technicians
Social class VI   —   skilled manual wage-workers with completed apprenticeships
Social class VII —   semi- and unskilled manual workers and agricultural workers
This listing is taken from Heath (1981, p. 52). For more precise details see Goldthorpe (1980).
Source: Heath, 1981, table 2.1.

In this chapter, we have explored the way in which the capitalist productive process shapes social classes, occupational groupings and stratification systems. However, in our discussion of the processes associated with the creation of the economic surplus, we have given little attention to the manner in which this is distributed. Some, of course, will be reinvested in the productive process for the purposes of further technological innovation and for extending the scale of output. But, at the same time, other parts of the surplus will be paid as taxes to the state, and as interest on loans and as dividends to shareholders. A large number of companies remain 'private' and are owned by a limited number of individual shareholders. These tend to be relatively small businesses, in terms of both the number of their employees and their levels of trading. But with the growth of large-scale, joint-stock companies operating in national and international markets, the nature of their ownership has changed. While the significance of individual shareholders has declined, there has been the growing preponderance of institutional stockholders (Scott, 1979). In Britain, for instance, as table 2 illustrates, the proportion of the market value of company shares held by individuals has fallen from 54.0 per cent in 1963 to 37.5 per cent in 1975.

It is the intervention of pension funds and insurance companies that largely accounts for the increase in institutional shareholdings

TABLE 2   OWNERSHIP OF COMPANY SHARES IN THE
UNITED KINGDOM, 1963–75

Type of shareholder	% of market value held		
	1963	1969	1975
Personal	54.0	47.4	37.5
Insurance companies	10.0	12.2	15.9
Pension funds	6.4	9.0	16.8
Unit trusts	1.3	2.9	4.1
Investment trusts	10.0	8.7	10.0
Banks	1.3	1.7	0.7
Total	83.0	81.9	85.0

Source: Scott, 1979, table 26.

as a result of their investment policies, which are determined by their need to meet the economic interests of their policyholders and subscribers. But who are these policyholders and subscribers? To an overwhelming extent they are managerial, professional and other higher-grade employees who own insurance policies and who contribute to occupationally related pension funds. Accordingly, the middle class benefits from the capitalist accumulation process in two ways. First, within the sphere of production, they receive high salaries. Second, within the sphere of distribution, they obtain further income through their claims on pension funds and insurance policies. By contrast, those producing the economic surplus – the working class – receive relatively low earnings within the sphere of production and little within the sphere of distribution. This is notwithstanding the fact that some productive workers do own insurance policies and that many trade unions have pension funds that invest in capitalist-owned corporations.

However, the state also acquires revenue from capitalist corporations through its collection of taxes. Although most of this is used for education, health, welfare and defence expenditure, some is directly reinvested into the productive process, into either state-owned nationalised or capitalist corporations. In general, the state has been directly involved in the productive process in all capitalist countries during the post-war decades. This is not least because of a fall in profits and the subsequent inability of capitalist corporations to raise privately owned finance for the purposes of reinvestment (Himmelstrand et al., 1981). For this reason, the state has become either a minority or majority shareholder in corporations engaged in a wide range of productive and service activities. This was very much the trend during the 1970s in most of the Western European countries. It has, to some extent, been halted in the 1980s. Additionally, the state continues to fulfil its traditional role of providing the necessary conditions for the operation of capitalist corporations. Privately owned businesses cannot function without an agency that will guarantee a legal framework, stable currency, markets, and a supply of suitably qualified labour.

The growth of state services during the twentieth century has increased the proportion of public sector employees in the occupational structures of the capitalist countries (Scase, 1980). How are these to be allocated within the class structure, bearing in mind that classes are shaped by the social relations of production? In state-owned productive enterprises – such as, for example, the nationalised industries – it is possible to identify occupations associated with the functions of control and coordination, development and planning, and the execution of work tasks just as in any privately owned capitalist corporation. In state-owned unproductive institutions, however, the situation is rather different. At first sight, the class positions of nurses, school teachers and local government officers, for example, do not appear to be directly related to the functions associated with the production of an economic surplus. But indirectly they are related to the capitalist productive process. Many occupations within the state or public sector contribute to the efficient operation of the accumulation process. The functions of state employees associated with a variety of tasks – ranging from housing, health, welfare, education to technological research – may be interpreted in this way.

Furthermore, the organisation of work tasks within the state sector may reflect that of the typical capitalist corporation. Thus it is possible to identify those in occupations mainly associated with the functions of coordination and control and those who follow instructions and are involved in the execution of work tasks. Within a state-owned hospital, for example, there are, on the one hand, doctors, surgeons, administrators and planners; on the other, there are nurses, canteen assistants and ward orderlies. Similarly, within local government bureaucracies, there are chief executives, managers and administrators responsible for coordinating and controlling the execution of work tasks undertaken by others. Therefore, even outside the capitalist productive process proper, there exist the conditions for the emergence of class relationships.

The object of this chapter has been to outline the essential characteristics of the capitalist mode of production. We have outlined the major features of the productive process and how this shapes the broad contours of social relations. On this basis, we have located social classes, occupational groupings and systems of social stratification. However, although these are inherent features of the capitalist mode of production, their expression will vary between countries according to different socio-political and historical circumstances. We consider some of these in the next chapter.

3

Contrasts in Capitalism:
National Differences

In the previous chapter we have outlined the core features of the
capitalist mode of production and described the manner in which
this generates class relationships, occupational structures and systems
of social stratification. All capitalist societies can be described in
these terms. Nevertheless, the expression of these processes may
differ between countries. Although, for example, there is always
wage-labour and capital, the relative strength of these forces in
shaping inequalities will vary. Similarly, the role of the state as
an intermediary between classes and as an instrument of social
reform differs in a variety of ways. It is the task of this chapter
to explore the many contrasts that exist between different Western
capitalist countries.

There are many variations between these countries in the structure and composition of capital ownership. They derive, first, from
the nature of the interrelationship between different 'types' of
capital, and secondly, from the extent to which capital has become
monopolised. It is, therefore, possible to distinguish between, for
example agrarian, industrial and financial capital and to investigate
the manner in which they are interrelated in different countries.
(By these distinctions we mean simply to refer to financial and
commercial interests structured within the spheres of agriculture,
commerce and industrial manufacturing.) In some countries agriculture provided the finance for industrial development, and many
landowners became capitalist entrepreneurs. In Sweden, the early
industries were founded in the *bruks* of the landed estates so that
agrarian and industrial capital developed in close relationship.[1] In

the United States, by contrast, early industrialisation occurred over an ever-expanding territory within which industrial and agricultural interests were often sharply divided. In Britain, although aristocratic and agrarian interests were involved in the development of industries, on the whole their investment was primarily directed towards commerce, trade and finance rather than to manufacturing.

If we compare the composition of capital in Britain with that of other countries, there is a greater divide between the financial and industrial sectors (Glyn and Sutcliffe, 1972). Unlike those in the Scandinavian countries, and Germany and France, British banks do not generally undertake long-term investment in industrial enterprises. They are more likely to make short-term loans and to play a passive role in any function of ownership. Financial institutions in Britain – the banks, insurance companies and the City of London institutions – have tended to invest in property and commerce either in Britain or overseas. This has meant that manufacturing companies have not had the same access to funds for investment as have corporations in, say, France or Germany. Indeed, the division between financial and industrial capital interests in Britain is reflected in conflicts over such matters as the value of the currency and the level of interest rates. The needs of manufacturing capital are normally best served by a low rate of interest on borrowing, those of finance by the reverse conditions. Indeed, it has been argued that one of the major factors that accounts for the poor growth rate of British manufacturing industry is the influence that financial institutions have been able to exercise over the Treasury in order to ensure that governments pursue monetary and economic policies which favour financial rather than manufacturing interests (Scott, 1979). In France and Western Germany, by contrast, the greater degree of integration between finance and manufacturing capital has meant that the banks and other financial institutions – as active and long-term shareholders in industrial corporations – have provided resources, often in conjunction with the state, for investment, technological modernisation and, hence, economic growth (Birnbaum, 1980).

A further way in which the structure of capital varies between countries is in its degree of monopolisation. In some, industrial resources are highly concentrated within a limited number of corporations, while in others there is a relatively large proportion of small-scale, non-monopoly enterprises. The monopolistic tendency of capitalism has had important implications for the nature of occupational structures. While the proportion of manual workers has declined in the advanced capitalist countries, the growth of large-scale corporations has led to an increase in the demand for managerial, professional, technical and white-collar employees (Noble, 1981; Westergaard and Resler, 1975). Similarly, the growth of these large-scale capitalist enterprises has reduced the number of business proprietors. In Britain, for example, where the decline has been the most dramatic, they have declined by 50 per cent since 1911 (Brown, 1978). The growth of monopoly capital has led to the demise of small-scale productive and distributive units and hence of the petty bourgeoisie as a social stratum. The expanding ranks of administrative, professional and technical employees – those fulfilling the functions of capital within the productive process – now constitute the core of a large, corporate-based middle class.

The growth of large-scale corporations is confirmed by developments in the United Kingdom. Although at the turn of the century, the 100 largest manufacturing firms accounted for 15 per cent of total net output, their share had increased to 50 per cent by the mid-1970s (Hannah and Kay, 1977). Similarly, there has been a growing concentration of ownership: by the late 1960s, the 100 largest firms owned 75 per cent of the net assets held by publicly quoted companies (Hannah, 1975). The twentieth century, then, has witnessed the concentration of manufacturing through the process of mergers, takeovers and amalgamations rather than through indigenous company growth (Hannah, 1975).

However, the increasing concentration of economic production – although the dominant trend in capitalist countries – has been far from uniform. There are important variations both *within* and *between* countries. Some economic sectors typically have high levels of industrial concentration; in these so-called advanced branches, fixed capital expenditure tends to be very high. The dominance of a handful of highly capitalised multinational companies in the petrochemical industry, for example, is well known. A similar situation exists in many other industrial sectors, especially in the chemical and allied trades, electrical engineering, the manufacture of electrical goods, vehicles, and iron and steel (Utton, 1970). By contrast, small firms predominate in those sectors that produce

specialised technical products, craft-based commodities and luxury
consumer goods (Wilson Committee, 1979). These, together with
the labour-intensive personal service sector, are the main contexts
for the formation and growth of small businesses (Scase and Goffee,
1982). To over-generalise about the impact of monopoly capital,
therefore, is to neglect key sectors of the capitalist economy within
which small-scale systems of production, work and organisation
persist.

The continuing importance of small-scale enterprises and their
varying importance in different countries is indicated in table 3.

TABLE 3   THE CONTRIBUTION TO EMPLOYMENT IN
MANUFACTURING OF SMALL ENTERPRISES
(WITH LESS THAN 200 EMPLOYEES)
IN SELECTED WEST EUROPEAN COUNTRIES

	(%)
Denmark (1973)	52.1
Italy (1971)	47.3
West Germany (1970)	37.0
France (1976)	34.2
United Kingdom (1976)	22.6

Source: Boissevain, 1980, table 2

The importance of small businesses in the manufacturing sector
is greater, for example, in Italy than in Britain. In Western
Germany and France more than one-third of all manufacturing
employment is provided by businesses with fewer than 200 employees.
Britain is exceptional in having such a low proportion of industrial-
manufacturing workers in small-scale enterprises. However, it seems
that there are a number of factors that account for the persistence
of small businesses. There are, in all capitalist countries, traditional
industrial sectors within which the persistence of craft skills, a
low level of technology and the limited requirements for finance
encourage the formation of small-scale enterprises (Scase and Goffee,
1980). In the British printing industry, for instance, there is a legacy
of craftsmen starting their own businesses.

The growth of large-scale corporations utilising mass production and assembly-line techniques has, in most capitalist countries, also encouraged the formation of small firms through sub-contracting the manufacture of specialist components (Friedman, 1977). In this way, large corporations have been able to avoid some of the costs of production since small sub-contractors bear the expense of setting up specialised productive techniques and, at the same time, employ cheaper, non-unionised labour. In this manner, small firms which are technically and financially autonomous are often in fact little more than subsidiaries, heavily dependent upon the requirements of large corporations for their survival. Further, some economic sectors within capitalist countries will always be labour-intensive. These are the bases for the formation and growth of small firms if only because of the low level of capital required for starting small businesses (Scase and Goffee, 1980).

Finally, in all capitalist countries there are industrial sectors within which new technologies are encouraging the formation of small businesses. In computing and microelectronics, recent advances have reduced the cost of many labour-saving devices so that more small businesses can afford to lease or purchase data-processing equipment. The mini and micro computer, for instance, allow relatively sophisticated software to be used by non-specialist staff. All these factors favouring the starting of small businesses may contribute to an increasing disenchantment with work in large-scale productive systems and a decline in formal employment in different capitalist countries. Scientists and research staff in large-scale organisations within which their career prospects are highly limited can often start 'high-tech' small firms as an expression of personal job dissatisfaction.

It is difficult to determine why the role of small firms in manufacturing should vary so much between countries. Most important among a number of possible factors are differences in the roles of the state. The growth of the welfare state has involved manpower planning, an increase in the social wage and an extension of control over the market such that the conditions for small-business growth have deteriorated. Even if small enterprises are encouraged by governments, this support is unlikely to reverse capitalism's inherent monopolistic tendency. Even so, the political impact of the petty bourgeoisie will continue to be felt in all capitalist countries. Their commitment to private property, the market, risk-taking and profit help to legitimate the capitalist dynamic within which monopoly and quasi-monopoly corporations can flourish (Bechhofer and Elliott, 1981). In France, for example, the petty bourgeoisie has been important in shaping the nature of political debate and the electoral success of political parties. In this way, the petty bourgeoisie is more important than its economic position under the conditions of monopoly capital would suggest.

In this chapter, so far, we have discussed the manner in which the composition of capital – large and small – varies between countries. In a similar manner, national states differ in their relationships to capital and their regulation of the productive process. However, it is first necessary to outline the essential characteristics of the state in capitalist society. It will then be possible to consider national differences.

There are two approaches to the study of the state in capitalist society: the 'liberal-democratic' and the 'Marxist'.[2] Briefly, liberal-democratic theories consider the state to consist of an autonomous set of institutions, politically neutral and distanced from the interests of any single economic and social force. It is 'up for grabs', to be used by democratically elected regimes to administer their mandated policies. Within this perspective, the state is seen as necessary for enforcing the rules within which socio-economic interests pursue their objectives. It is, further, regarded as the institutional base for the 'political' as distinct from the 'economic' sphere. Consequently, this view assumes that capitalist countries are structurally separated and that the 'political' is irreducible to the 'economic'. This is seen to be one of the major differences between capitalist and East European countries: in the latter, the two are fused, creating essentially totalitarian social structures.

The Marxist approach starts with the claim that the state is an instrument of capital.[3] Therefore, the development of various state activities can only be explained by reference to the requirements of capital. In the case of increasing state intervention in housing, education, urban planning, health and welfare, for example, this is seen to be a result of capital's need for a healthy, literate and efficient workforce. Any changes in state provision in these areas are explained by reference to the requirements of capital. Of course, the state in any capitalist country has to meet certain basic needs of capital. It has to provide satisfactory conditions for capital accumulation, otherwise the essential dynamic underlying economic production would falter. Thus any state has to provide the following minimum conditions. First, a legal framework that guarantees a market for the exchange of commodities and labour, and the general regulation of trade. Second, a stable currency and a regulated monetary system. Third, a supply of labour for the capitalist enterprise. Finally, the state must protect private property and be responsible for law and order.

To describe these minimum conditions is not to assume that there will always be a direct fit between the needs of capital and the activities of the state. A major shortcoming of many Marxist analyses is that they neglect tensions and contradictions between capital and the state (Parkin, 1971). These often arise from divisions and cleavages within the composition of capital which is fragmented into large-scale multinational companies and small businesses, agrarian and industrial enterprises, and financial and industrial corporations. Although the state has to meet the needs of capital *in general*, in practice it must deal with the competing interests of these different sectors. It is only when the state is removed from a direct relationship with any particular sector that it can provide the necessary conditions for capitalist production *in general*. It is for this reason that many Marxists have argued that the state must have 'relative autonomy' and, by definition, be distanced from the direct control of capital (Poulantzas, 1972). Hence, they claim that the role of the state can vary between capitalist countries and can shape their respective social structures in distinctive ways. This will depend upon a range of economic, social and political forces as they operate within different countries.

We may illustrate this by reference to a particular need of capital: the requirement for labour. One of the conditions for capitalist production is the existence of formally free workers who sell their labour as a commodity in the market. This is a universal feature of the capitalist mode of production. However, the conditions under which this labour is exchanged for a wage are determined not only by capital, but also by the state. The state's relative autonomy allows it to choose, for example, between various manpower policies. So during the growth decades of the 1950s and 1960s, different national states in Western countries coped with labour shortages in a number of ways: by encouraging the permanent immigration of workers and their families, by issuing short-term work and residence permits for migrants, and by encouraging 'marginal' workers – for example, women and the partially disabled – to participate in the labour market. In Western Germany, for example, the state regulated the supply of migrant labour through the issue of short-term residence permits, while in Sweden labour shortages were overcome both by regulated immigration from Southern Europe and by encouraging the greater work participation of women. Similarly, differences exist between countries in the extent to which the state directly intervenes in the employment relationship, industrial relations and wage-bargaining systems, and in the provision of social welfare (Strinati, 1982).

Clearly, the needs of capital are important in shaping the role of the state. But there are also other factors that need to be taken into account, especially the influence of organised labour. It is within this context that any discussion of the state needs to consider the nature of political regimes as the expression of specific interests. It is, for example, through the election of social democratic governments that working-class organisations can steer the state in the direction of their interests. This can lead to legislation which extends the rights of employees in such areas as employment protection, health and safety at work, redundancy, industrial retraining and so on. While this may not change the essentially antagonistic and exploitative relationship between wage labour and capital, workers' material circumstances may be improved. One needs only to compare the rights of Swedish workers with those of black workers in South Africa to recognise this point.

But such 'reformism' does have its costs for the capitalist enterprise. Profit margins may be severely reduced by additional costs created by redundancy legislation and the implementation of state-imposed health and safety regulations. When an increase in production costs of this sort cannot be passed on by raising prices, the essential dynamic of the capitalist productive process is challenged. We must, therefore, avoid making too sharp a distinction between reformism, which is geared to change *within* the system, and forms of radicalism, which are explicity geared to system transformation. Thus organised labour and social democratic regimes can implement reforms so that capitalist corporations no longer perceive particular countries as offering favourable conditions for production. In these circumstances, when profits are low, the state may intervene directly in the productive process in order to provide funds for investment, modernisation and employment. The development of nationalised industries, state subsidies and state-owned capitalist enterprises in most Western European countries can be explained in these terms. This was particularly the case in Western Europe during the late 1960s and the 1970s when governments often intervened in the ownership of companies in order to prevent plant closures and to strive to maintain 'full' employment. Reformism, then, may create state capitalism and may also encourage the flight of multinational capital to less developed countries (attractive on account of low wages and the absence of social security systems, of effective trade unionism and of well-organised labour movements).

If we are to compare national states, it is possible to identify a number of common trends in their development. First, the state has increasingly taken responsibility for the maintenance and reproduction of the labour force in such matters as education, occupational training, housing, health and welfare. Second, it has assumed greater powers in the maintenance of social order. Occupational change and the rationalisation of the productive process have created high rates of labour mobility. This, in turn, has destroyed many of the informal, community-based sources of social control and has encouraged the state to implement more formal mechanisms (Harrison, 1983). Third, the functions of the state have become more centralised. In every capitalist country there have been attempts to integrate local and regional state activities into centralised, national bureaucracies. This is evident within most branches of the state, ranging from education and social welfare to, paradoxically, regional economic planning (Hirsch, 1980). Fourth, a general crisis of profitability has brought about a greater degree of state intervention within the productive process (Jessop, 1980). Even the 1979 and 1983 elected Conservative governments in Britain, committed to reducing the state's role within the economy, have been unable to reverse fundamentally this interventionist trend. (This is despite the sale or 'privatisation' of certain 'key' state-owned companies by the Thatcher government during the 1980s.) Finally, the autonomy of national states has been reduced by the growth of multinational corporations and the concomitant internationalisation of world trade. Within an international division of labour, the peripheral states – those of underdeveloped and developing countries – have become increasingly dependent upon the central capitalist countries of Western Europe and the United States.

National states, however, also exhibit enduring differences which are an expression of the social, political and economic forces found in each country. There are, for instance, variations in the extent to which state activities are centralised within national bureaucratic structures rather than undertaken by municipal and regional bodies. In Italy, for example, the administrative system is highly decentralised and tightly enmeshed in complex patterns of local political and economic relationships (Donolo, 1980). Decision-making tends to rely upon an elaborate system of patron–client relationships which serve to integrate the local, regional and national levels of the political system. In France, on the other hand, centralisation reinforces the strong and autonomous state which has been able to develop a system of national economic planning within which capitalist objectives are constrained (Birnbaum, 1980). Corporatism, as a system of public control over privately owned assets, is accordingly more highly developed in France than in either Britain or Italy. Only in Sweden is corporatism so fully developed by virtue of a highly centralised state system (Himmelstrand et al., 1981).

This leads to a further difference: states in capitalist countries do not have equal autonomy from the interests of capital. In Sweden, a strong working-class movement has elected a succession of Social Democrat governments which have wrested the state from domination by purely capitalist interests and used it as an instrument to pursue many working-class interests. By contrast, the states in less developed capitalist countries such as Greece and Spain have less autonomy from capital if only because industrialisation and economic growth have been dependent upon foreign-based finance (Mouzelis, 1978). Such states are far more vulnerable to the international movement of capital than those states of the industrially more mature countries. More specifically, they are in competition with each other in attracting capital for industrial investment. With the economic recession of the 1980s, this dependency is becoming a feature of the weaker industrial economies such as those of Britain, Denmark and Ireland.

A further difference between national states is the extent to which

they have intervened in the labour market and in the regulation
of industrial relations. In Britain attempts by the state to control
wages have often met with resistance because of traditions of 'free',
decentralised collective bargaining at the plant level (Strinati, 1982).
In West Germany, by contrast, where the industrial relations system
is more centralised, state guidelines on economic planning have
been more readily accepted. However, any comparative analysis
of the role of the state must take into account the traditions and
relative strength of working-class movements.

The composition of the working classes of the different capitalist
countries is the first important consideration. In some countries
it is characterised by a high degree of homogeneity, while in others
there are marked sources of division. Many of these are related
to the development of capitalism and the manner in which this has
shaped industrial and occupational structures. In Sweden the
comparatively recent development of monopoly capital has produced
a more homogeneous working class than in Britain, Italy or France
(Korpi, 1983). In Sweden there is a relative absence of divisions
within the working class relating to such factors as craft, trade and
skill. Consequently, its more recent industrialisation, based upon
the demand for semi-skilled industrial workers, has limited the
emergence of sharp cleavages of the kind found in many other
countries. In other countries, by contrast, the formation of craft
unions within early capitalism has continued to affect working-class
industrial and political organisations. Trade unionism in Britain,
for example, has institutionalised sharp distinctions between craft
and semi-skilled workers, fostering a preoccupation with differentials
in wage-bargaining. As a result, the potential for the formation
of a class-based union movement that can pursue the interests of
all employees is weakened (Scase, 1977; Stephens, 1979).

A further consideration is the trajectory of industrialisation. The
effect of this on the composition of different working classes is seen
in terms of divisions relating to industry, region and scale of enterprise. In France, Italy and Spain, for instance, the high proportion
of small businesses, combined with a large agricultural sector and
a low level of industrial concentration, have impeded the development of class-based institutions and consciousness. The development
of monopoly capital, because of its standardising effects, may reduce
the relevance of these traditional divisions in the future. However,

there are also other sources of cleavage that need to be taken into account. Capital's demand for labour during the 1950s and 1960s has created new populations of 'migrant' or 'immigrant' workers in most European countries: in France, Algerian and Portuguese workers; in Western Germany, Turkish and Yugoslav migrants; in Britain, immigrants from former colonial territories. In each case, trade unions and working-class parties have done little to represent the interests of these new industrial workers, who have largely become a sub-strata within the different working classes (Moore, 1977). In other words, they possess only a minimum of legal, social, political and economic rights, concentrated as they are in the worst housing and the lowest-paid occupations. Similarly, capital's demand for cheap labour has been expressed in the increased participation rate of women in the labour market (Oakley, 1981). This has done little to reduce gender-based inequalities and prejudices within male-dominated corporations and labour unionism.

Clearly, the presence or absence of divisions among workers will affect the extent to which working-class movements can change the structure of society. Sweden is exceptional among capitalist countries in having a political party and trade unions which, together, operate as a class-based movement (Korpi, 1983; Scase, 1977). Elsewhere, trade unions are vehicles of particular occupational, industrial and craft divisions; as such, they fail to express effectively working-class interests. As a result, and alternatively, these interests may be pursued through the formation of social democratic parties. Clearly, these have achieved a far greater degree of electoral support in some countries than in others. While in the Scandinavian countries, for example, there are now well-established social democratic traditions, this is not the case in West Germany, Italy or France, despite some recent successes (Korpi, 1983). But have social democratic regimes had a significant impact upon social structures? The question may be answered by reference to a general comparison of West European countries and, within this context, by a more detailed analysis of the Scandinavian countries which provide useful test cases for assessing the effects of social democratic regimes.

Of the countries in Western Europe, Norway and Sweden have strong traditions of social democratic or labour regimes. The achievements of these parties have been outstanding in the extent to which they have been able to retain control over the governmental apparatus for sustained periods of time during the post-war era (Korpi, 1983). Indeed, in each of these two countries, the political impact of the working-class party had already become well established during the 1930s. In the other countries of Western Europe, social democratic and labour parties have been far less successful in wielding political power. When they have enjoyed periods of government they have either been severely constrained as 'minority' regimes or as the participants in more broadly based coalitions. This has generally been the pattern in such countries as Denmark, Holland, Belgium, France and Western Germany. Indeed, it is only in Austria and Britain that labour parties have been able to form majority governments for any substantial periods of time. Even so, the British and Austrian labour parties have been unable to enjoy a level of political ascendancy comparable to that of the social democratic parties of Norway and Sweden (Castles, 1978).

However, a distinction needs to be made between the Austrian and British cases on the one hand and the Swedish and Norwegian on the other. Despite the fact that Britain and Austria have had experience of majority labour governments, the political parties compete within two-party electoral systems. This is not the case for the other social democratic parties of Norway and Sweden. Accordingly, there has often been a tendency for the Austrian and British parties to take second place to conservative parties, while in the Scandinavian countries the social democratic parties confront fragmented oppositions in multi-party political systems. The Scandinavian countries may, therefore, be considered more social democratic than either Britain or Austria, since, although the latter have a track record of labour regimes, the overall political ascendancy of these parties tends to be far less. Certainly, in Sweden and Norway the margin of electoral support for the Social Democrats over the next largest party is far greater. In no other countries have social democratic parties had such continuous success over their political rivals (Korpi, 1983). But what have these two parties achieved in improving the economic and social conditions of their working-class supporters?

Castles has attempted to assess the effects of social democratic policies for the development of welfare systems by constructing an 'index of welfare state provision' (Castles, 1978). This is based upon four separate indicators. First, government revenue as a percentage of gross domestic product. This is used because it indicates the extent to which governments choose to determine the allocation of national economic resources. A high level of government revenue is a necessary precondition for state-financed welfare systems. Second, total public spending on education as a percentage of gross national product. This component is included because education can be considered to be an institutional expression of citizenship rights; an extension of educational provision potentially offers a broadened gateway for economic, cultural and social improvement. Third, infant mortality as measured in terms of deaths per thousand live births. This is included on the assumption that these rates are a measure of the general health, welfare and living conditions of a population. Finally, gross domestic product per capita. This is a measure of national wealth rather than welfare, but it does have important welfare implications; without the creation of wealth, living standards cannot be improved. The averages of each of these four indices constitute Castles' 'index of welfare state provision'. The 'scores' that he calculates for a selected number of countries are listed in table 4.[4]

Table 4 is drawn from a broader analysis of OECD countries and from this it is striking that Sweden, Norway, Denmark and the Netherlands are far ahead of all the other countries in their

TABLE 4   INDEX OF STATE WELFARE PROVISION FOR SELECTED WEST EUROPEAN COUNTRIES IN THE MID-1970s

Country	Index of welfare state provision
Sweden	93
Norway	85
Netherlands	82
Denmark	80
France	50
United Kingdom	39
West Germany	36
Austria	23

Source: Extracted from Castles, 1978, table 2.4

level of welfare provision; indeed, the major cleavage is between these countries and the rest. Thus it would seem that the social democratic regimes of Norway and Sweden have had a particular impact upon the development of state welfare systems. Perhaps the Netherlands is an anomaly since it has no social democratic traditions of the Scandinavian kind. Even so, this should not detract from the high level of state welfare provision in the Scandinavian countries.

Although state welfare systems may ameliorate economic disadvantages through improvements in housing, health and social insurance, they are but one mechanism of social reform. It is also possible that social democratic regimes will tackle inequalities in opportunity and reward. How far, then, have the Scandinavian countries higher rates of upward social mobility and more egalitarian income distributions than other countries? Most social democratic governments have attempted to improve opportunities for working-class children through reforms of the educational system. In Norway and Sweden, for example, there has been the introduction of non-streamed comprehensive schooling. Similarly, higher education has been reformed in order to expand opportunities for part-time study and to provide 'second chances' for those already in the labour market. There has, in other words, been a rapid expansion of continuing education in the universities of the Scandinavian countries.

However, these changes are not unique to these social democratic countries; in most of Western Europe – irrespective of political regime – comprehensive education systems have been introduced and provision for adult higher education expanded. However, and very significantly, such reforms appear to have achieved little in improving the mobility chances of working-class youth in the occupational structure. As stated in the previous chapter, with the development of capitalism, occupational structures have become increasingly polarised between a minority of managerial and professional occupations and all others. Perhaps, then, the appropriate measure of the 'openness' of class structures is the pattern of recruitment into these occupations rather than movement between manual and non-manual jobs.[5] Sociologists have traditionally paid more attention to the latter because of difficulties in determining the composition of elites; problems which are compounded in comparative analyses.

But if we do consider patterns of recruitment into elite occupations, the chances of manual working-class children seem to be not as great in Sweden – for which there is substantial and reliable evidence – as in Britain or, for that matter, the United States. ('Elite' in mobility studies normally refers to higher-grade managerial and professional positions in both public and private sectors.) According to Heath, approximately 43 per cent of the elite in Sweden is recruited from working-class manual backgrounds, the figure for Britain is 49 per cent; West Germany 34 per cent; and the United States 54 per cent (Heath, 1981, table 7.4). Indeed, inequalities of opportunity in Sweden have been highlighted by Erikson, who found that the sons of civil servants have about thirteen times the chances of obtaining an elite occupation compared with those of manual workers. Even the sons of lower-grade white-collar workers have more than six times the chances of obtaining such positions than those of manual employees (Erikson, 1976).

Within economies that are overwhelmingly privately owned, it is difficult to envisage how recruitment into the more highly rewarded occupations can be 'democratised' by reformist governments without increasing the level of direct state intervention in the economy. Until such a time, recruitment into 'top' positions is going to depend largely upon the requirements and preferences of corporate executives who may be far from committed to social democratic ideals of equality. Indeed, two consequences can possibly follow from a broadening of educational opportunity, especially in the stagnant economies of the 1980s. First, as education becomes more widespread, it might take more of it to 'buy' a given occupation than was formerly the case. (In other words, university degrees may become prerequisites for certain occupations where previously school-leaving qualifications were sufficient.) Second, more prevalent higher education may encourage corporate leaders to consider non-meritocratic criteria such as 'character', 'breadth of vision' and 'quality of leadership'. Such considerations may operate – implicitly if not explicitly – against the selection of children from working-class backgrounds. Indeed, it is for such 'alleged' processes that Britain is often seen to be an extremely 'class'- or status-ridden society.

It is, then, difficult to envisage how social democratic regimes can broaden patterns of occupational recruitment by solely educational reforms and without more direct intervention in the labour market. This, in fact, highlights a major dilemma confronting all social democratic regimes in capitalist countries. They may be ideologically committed to meritocratic and even egalitarian aims, but they often attempt to achieve these within the context of capitalist-owned economic systems. However, this is not to dismiss entirely social democratic efforts to democratise educational systems – such changes do improve the competitive position of qualified working-class youth within the labour market. The point is that because of the selectivity exercised by companies and other institutions, many of the ambitions of technically qualified youth will remain unfulfilled. Working-class frustration and resentment can, therefore, be a significant consequence of expanded educational provision in a capitalist society.

If social democratic regimes appear to have had relatively little effect on patterns of elite recruitment, the same seems to apply to their egalitarian economic aims. Certainly, there is little evidence of any fundamental changes in the position of industrial manual workers in comparison with those of other occupational groups. In a comparative analysis of income differentials in Norway, Denmark and Sweden in which he examined the distribution of household incomes in terms of the proportion received by each tenth of the population, Uusitalo (1975) found that the distribution of income in each of these countries was extremely unequal. Thus the highest 10 per cent received an income share which was up to three times greater than it would receive if the distribution were completely unequal. Correspondingly, the lowest 10 per cent obtained only a fifth of the share it would receive in the case of complete equality. Further, income per capita was from eight to fifteen times greater in the highest tenth of the population than in the lowest.

However, such evidence should not lead us to assume necessarily that social democratic regimes have had no effect on patterns of income inequality. Although they appear to have brought about no *fundamental* changes within overall patterns of rewards, they have often introduced tax systems which have brought about a shift towards greater equality. Table 3 suggests this to be the case for the social democratic countries of Norway and Sweden but not for France and West Germany. This would seem to be only partly a result of social democratic policies, for the table also indicates a shift towards equality in the Netherlands.

TABLE 5   PERCENTAGE OF TOTAL INCOME RECEIVED
BY THE HIGHEST 20 PER CENT OF HOUSEHOLDS IN
SELECTED WEST EUROPEAN COUNTRIES IN THE 1970s

	Before tax	*After tax*
France	47.0	47.1
West Germany	46.8	46.3
Netherlands	45.8	36.3
Norway	40.9	37.7
Sweden	40.5	35.0
United Kingdom	40.3	39.3

Source: Extracted from Sawyer, 1976, table 3

Any explanation which accounts for the general persistence of fundamental inequalities must acknowledge the extent to which social democratic governments have little power to alter processes which are essentially determined by the capitalist market. They may be able to modify patterns of income distribution through state-imposed systems of progressive taxation but they are unable to attack the root causes. Even Castles, an unswerving enthusiast of the social democratic cause, is forced to admit that 'The gap between those who receive very high incomes or possess considerable wealth and the rest of society might aptly be described as the "unpleasant face of social democracy"' (1978, p. 88). So the social democratic strategy seems to require a compromise in which the owners and controllers of capital retain most of their economic privileges. The gap between them and others is woven into the very fabric of the political and economic system. Accordingly, there would seem to be an inescapable contradiction between the aims of social democratic governments and those of capitalism.

It would appear, then, to be difficult to differentiate *in any fundamental manner* between capitalist societies according to their experience of social democratic regimes. Perhaps such a conclusion, however, is rather too sweeping in view of the ways in which working-class organisations have been able to affect the general conditions under which capitalist production takes place. In addition to the implementation of policies which have improved general levels of social welfare, one of the major institutional achievements of social democratic regimes has been the introduction of laws which have limited and constrained the activities of capitalist corporations. In Swedish companies, for example, laws protect workers' interests in decision-making, job security and the quality of the working environment. The boards of companies with more than 100 employees must include trade union representatives, and there have been attempts to democratise privately owned corporations by increasing the level of trade union participation in company planning (Himmelstrand et al., 1981). In matters of this kind, Swedish manual workers are in a more favourable position than their counterparts in most other capitalist countries. Further, through trade union organisations, their interests are represented on the National Labour Board, which is probably the most influential of all Swedish economic institutions (Jones, 1976). In many ways, it represents the limits to which an economy can be planned and controlled without the direct abolition of capitalist ownership. It is central to the operations of the capitalist dynamic if only because it is directly involved in most aspects of manpower planning, occupational training, employment services, industrial location, economic forecasting and the manipulation of fiscal and economic resources for full employment and sustained economic growth.

It is because of such developments – and there are parallels in Norway – that it should not be assumed that the balance of power between capital and labour in various Western countries is identical. Although, by definition, each of these countries is organised around the principle of capital accumulation within which the economic surplus is appropriated by private owners, this does not rule out important differences in the representation of working-class interests within capitalist systems (Korpi, 1983; Scase, 1977). Further, it is not to assume that relationships between the state and the privately owned economy will be the same in all countries. The development of influential working-class movements in the social democratic countries - particularly, Norway and Sweden – has increased the representation of industrial manual workers, not only with capitalist corporations but also within state institutions (Korpi, 1983). This has reinforced the relative autonomy of the state and challenged the concentration of economic and political power. Although in the Scandinavian countries there are economic classes which own and control capital, it is doubtful whether these dominate the state apparatus to the same extent as in some other countries.

To this degree, social democratic governments have restricted the means whereby privately owned economic interests can monopolise political power (Stephens, 1979). They have not only improved the working and employment conditions of employees but also curtailed many traditional managerial prerogatives and enacted legislation which protects the interests of consumers, tenants and clients against many of the potential abuses of private and public bureaucracies. In these ways, therefore, the state has been used as an instrument for social reform. But since the state has also to provide the necessary conditions for capitalist production, it is riddled with contradictions – more so than in other capitalist countries where working-class interests are less influential (Himmelstrand et al., 1981).

There is, however, a further way in which social democracy creates contradictions within capitalist society; that is, in terms of an ideology that emphasises egalitarianism alongside a productive process that generates structural inequalities. This has led to resentment among working-class supporters of the labour movement. In Sweden, for example, various studies of workers' attitudes have shown that there is a greater awareness of social and economic inequalities than in many other countries (Scase, 1977; 1983). There also seems to be a shift to radicalism within the working class. As a result, the leadership of the Social Democratic Party and the labour unions are pursuing policies which, through state implementation, could challenge the nature of capitalism in Sweden and resolve many of the contradictions of social democracy in a capitalist country (Scase, 1983). These policies are linked to the creation of 'wage-earner funds' which would transfer economic ownership and control from private shareholders to union-based collectivities of wage-earners.[6] This would be achieved by forcing capitalist corporations to give shares to wage-earner funds in direct proportion to their gross profits. Twenty per cent of company profits would be issued as shares to these funds and in this way they would achieve a dominating control over large corporations within 15 to 20 years.

These funds would be administered by boards consisting of union officials and with some state representation.

If these proposals are implemented, they will enable a number of social democratic objectives to be fulfilled. First, they will attack the growing concentration of capitalist ownership and control. Second, they will provide a source of long-term capital funding which can be used for sustained publicly accountable investment. Third, they will avoid the over-centralisation of control which normally occurs in state-owned monopolies. Fourth, they will be a means to genuine industrial democracy. Finally, they will enable inequality to be attacked at its roots; that is, within the productive process. The Social Democratic government elected to office in 1982 is committed to implementing these proposals; if they are implemented, it will constitute a direct challenge to the nature of the capitalist mode of production in Sweden. Whether or not it will constitute a 'transition to socialism' is a matter for speculation (Korpi, 1983). Even so, developments in Sweden suggest that social democratic regimes, through their use of the state apparatus, can still be committed to challenging the capitalist dynamic. As such, there could yet be a parliamentary route to socialism (Stephens, 1979).

This chapter has attempted to highlight some of the differences that exist between capitalist countries, in order to emphasise that the capitalist mode of production does not impose complete uniformity upon various social structures. Because of an over-emphasis by observers upon its universal tendencies, the comparative study of national differences has often been neglected. We have focused upon the diversity of structures because this is crucial to any assessment of the future development of Western capitalist countries. But we can now introduce a further dimension into the analysis of industrial societies – that is, the comparison of capitalist and non-capitalist systems. Consequently, the questions concerning capitalist countries, their similarities and differences, which have been our approach in this part of the book, can now be applied in the same manner to the state socialist countries of Eastern Europe. Our analysis will hope to throw more light on both the universal and the specific relationships between the processes of productive labour, accumulation and the state, and their fundamental roles in shaping the social structures of the different countries.

Part II

The Analysis of State Socialism

4

The Development of
State Socialist Society

All three of the 'founding fathers' of modern sociology – Marx, Weber and Durkheim – were fascinated by the dynamics of class conflict in Europe and expected that working-class movements would play an important part in shaping the future direction of industrial societies. However, Marx had waited in vain for the revolutionary movements in Germany and France to attain political power, and Durkheim's alternative vision of a form of socialism based upon occupational associations was not to be realised.[1] Only Weber lived to witness the 1917 Bolshevik revolution in Russia; although fascinated by it, he was sceptical of its outcome. To him, it was not so much a radical movement to emancipate the working class as a form of dictatorship which would create a totalitarian bureaucracy in the name of socialism.[2] Marx, by contrast, had been optimistic about trade unions and workers' parties, believing that socialism offered the only solution to the inherent contradictions of capitalism. Only he, of the founding fathers, developed a theory of the transition from capitalism to socialism, but his blueprint for the future society was far from complete. Details of the more precise administrative, economic and political features of such a society were to be considered not by him, but by a later generation of Marxists, particularly Lenin, Trotsky and Bukharin.[3]

The essential features of present-day state socialist societies are both similar to and yet different from those of the capitalist countries. Both are complex industrial systems which are systematically geared to the accumulation of wealth. The accumulation process is organised in different ways and brings benefit to different sections of the population in the two types of society, but they have a common feature, namely that a proportion of economic output is not directly consumed and is available for the creation of further wealth. We have already described how, under capitalism, money capital (investment) is combined with labour, raw materials and machinery to create commodities which can be exchanged for a value greater than the costs involved in their production. This economic surplus becomes the property of the capitalist and it can then be used for self-enrichment in two ways: for private consumption or further investment for creating additional commodities and more wealth (chapter 2). We stressed that capitalism as a mode of production – as a socio-economic system and not just in the form of individual capital-owners and companies – is defined by the need to 'realise value', which is the search for profits by those who own and control the means of production. In the simplest form of capitalist accumulation, the incentive to invest comes directly from private individuals who own money and property or from groups of investors – shareholders – in joint-stock companies. In either case, capital is privately owned and production is for the private profit of the capitalist. Market mechanisms – the 'laws' of supply and demand – determine the prices of commodities, including labour, in the production process.

Seen as an abstract process, accumulation in state socialist societies has a similar form. Capital (money/investment) is put to work with the forces of production to create an economic surplus $(M \rightarrow C \rightarrow M_1)$ which is returned, in part at least, to the productive process in the form of new investment. The crucial difference between capitalism and state socialism is best illustrated by asking two questions: How is value realised? and Who gets the surplus? For capitalism, the answers are 'the market' and 'capitalists' respectively, and it is for this reason that the socialists have consistently fought to abolish private ownership of the means of production and to bring banks, credit, communications and transport under collective control. The state, therefore, provides money for investment which is applied to the productive process in ways which often resemble the capitalist pattern. Factories are built, wages are paid to workers and old machinery is continually replaced as under capitalism. One significant difference is that, under state socialism, investment has usually been more closely concentrated on developing a strong base of heavy industries – for example, energy extraction, steel and chemical production – rather than upon the manufacture of consumer goods. All but a very small fraction of this investment is monopolised by the state and it is guided by a centralised planning process instead of by individual capitalists' search for profit.

With hindsight, it is possible to see how far the transition from capitalist to 'socialist' industrialism in Russia and Eastern Europe conforms to this model. We will now trace this and consider the essential structural features which may be said to differentiate the 'socialist' from Western capitalist societies. We will first consider the circumstances of the Russian revolution and the emergence of the first socialist state. We will then describe the quite different circumstances under which state socialism was installed in the Eastern European countries after the Second World War. Although the general features of these societies have been a matter for considerable controversy between political parties as well as academic theorists, it is certain that they are neither capitalist nor a pure form of socialism. Our historically based account recognises the various interpretations which have stressed either similarities or differences in relation to capitalism, but steers a course between them.[4] We give equal weight to the facts of collective ownership and socialist ideology on the one hand and to the existence of highly centralised, one-party state apparatuses on the other. Hence our use of the term 'state socialist', which we will explain more fully in the course of our analysis.

To all appearances, and according to Marxist theory, Russia at the beginning of the twentieth century was not a likely candidate for a socialist revolution. After all, capitalism was under-developed and the proletariat was small and scattered. Imperial Russia was neither riven with the contradictions of mature capitalism nor divided into the 'two great camps' of the proletariat and bourgeoisie; in fact, 80 per cent of the population were peasants. The sharpest conflict was between modern liberalism and Tsarist autocracy as the new classes, especially the bourgeoisie, tried to free themselves from feudal institutions. However, it was not these internal movements but the First World War which brought the final blows to the old regime. The war with Germany on the western front was disastrous for Russia and it revealed the corruption and rigidity of the old regime and its lack of popular support.

In February 1917 came the first of the two revolutions of that year.[5] The intention of the social democrats who took power was to install a parliamentary system of the kind found in England or France; it was a 'bourgeois' revolution. In retrospect, it is easy to see why the elected Provisional Government could not last even a year. It was unable to guarantee Russia's defence or stability because it attracted only limited support from the workers and peasantry. Having come to power on a wave of popular discontent, as the military and economic situation continued to deteriorate, this short liberal-democratic phase was overwhelmed by the tide of events. It lasted as long as it did – eight months – only because the opposing revolutionary socialist groups were restrained by their belief, based on Marxist theory, that socialism could only develop out of the stage of *mature* capitalist economy.

As the social ferment grew, the demise of the Provisional Government became inevitable and it seemed that the path to political power was open to any party which could mobilise the support of both the peasantry and the urban working class. Between February and October 1917, workers, peasants and soldiers had formed a multitude of 'soviets', committees and other popular groupings, but they lacked a clear common purpose or direction. The Bolsheviks, with their slogan, 'peace, bread and land', through their consistent opposition to the Provisional Government and by skilful manoeuvring to gain the support of strategic groups, eventually emerged as the most coherent and most organised of the socialist parties. Consequently, on 25 October 1917, the Bolshevik Party, led by Lenin, carried out a successful military coup, and, in his words to the Petrograd Soviet, fulfilled the first condition for 'the building of the proletarian socialist state'.[6]

What did Lenin and the Bolsheviks have to do to achieve this goal? The problems were of two kinds: those which had to be faced by any revolutionary socialist movement and those which stemmed from the special circumstances of Russia in 1917. According to Marxist theories of the 'transition to socialism', the essential steps must be: first, the socialisation of land and property and an end to private accumulation and inheritance of wealth; second, the creation of new institutions for the democratic control of production, distribution and consumption; and third, a form of centralised proletarian state. In the aftermath of the October revolution, one can see the beginnings of this process of 'transition'. Even before the revolution, in fact, peasants had seized land from landlords and rich farmers; many factories were being run by workers' factory committees; and the army had ceased to function as an effective military organisation. At first, the Bolsheviks were content to go along with these largely spontaneous seizures of power by popular forces, and in some of their first decrees they nationalised land and key industries. Eventually, all but the smallest enterprises were nationalised. However, from the outset, the special conditions which prevailed in Russia began to shape the revolution in ways unforeseen by classical Marxist theory. Among these, the most important problems were the war and its disastrous effects on the economy, the political opposition (the Bolsheviks were a minority party even in the November 1917 Constituent Assembly), and the almost complete lack of an administrative infrastructure. In order to survive, let alone 'build socialism', the Bolsheviks had to make peace, consolidate their political power and rapidly rebuild the institutions needed for social and economic reconstruction.

Russia's war with Germany ended in March 1918 with a treaty giving away substantial areas of the territory on the western borders of the old Russian Empire. By this time, however, the revolutionary forces were facing a new military threat in the shape of foreign-assisted 'White Armies', led by former Tsarist officers. By 1921, the 'Whites' had been defeated by an increasingly large and effective Red Army which also provided the Bolshevik Party with one of its earliest means for enforcing centralised control. The significance of this period for the new regime's economic policy was the implementation of 'War Communism', which was dictated more by the sheer necessity of economic and military survival than by any utopian vision of socialism. Most of the earlier Bolshevik egalitarian decrees were reversed as the Soviet administration commandeered surplus food, regimented labour and acted as sole distributor of consumer goods.

The Bolsheviks had begun to consolidate their political position immediately after the revolution by forcibly disbanding the elected Constituent Assembly in order to build a system of administration under direct party control. It is in the period of War Communism that we find the origins of the unified party-state system which remains a typical feature of Eastern European state socialist societies.

The highly centralised rule of the Bolsheviks was further reinforced by the political police, the Cheka. Like its successor, the KGB, it was crucial for enforcing administrative decisions as well as for fighting counter-revolutionaries. In these tasks, it was responsible only to central party leaders.

From the outset, the Soviet system had the beginnings of a state framework which, in a developed form, persists today. Marxist theory envisaged a 'proletarian dictatorship' in the period of transition to socialism. It would be an intermediate phase in which the proletarian majority would need to exert its new-found power over the bouregois minority as it transformed the old institutions of state and society. Gradually, Marxists argued, the experience of work and administration in a socialist system and the lack of class antagonisms would allow the state to 'die away'. In the event, the popular revolutionary movements of 1917 did not lead to a 'class dictatorship' but, instead, rapidly crystallised into a 'dictatorial party-state'.[7] The leadership of the Russian Communist Party consolidated its rule through the party organisation, the army and the political police, so that whatever distance had existed between the party and the machinery of the state all but disappeared. In this way, it was able to monopolise all key areas of economic and political decision-making. Thus the foundations were laid for a process of capital accumulation of unprecedented speed.

The Soviet leadership, however, had first to arrest the disastrous economic decline which had started in 1914 and accelerated after the October revolution. By 1921, the rigours of War Communism had taken their toll on the loyalty of the urban industrial workers and the peasantry which had, in any case, always been reluctant to surrender surpluses of grain and other food to the central state administration. In a strategic retreat from socialist principles, the party leadership introduced the 'New Economic Policy' (NEP) in order to restore agricultural and industrial production to pre-war levels and to stabilise the currency. The NEP created a form of mixed economy in which the 'commanding heights' consisting of banks and large manufacturing enterprises would remain under public ownership while smaller enterprises and most of agriculture would be allowed to develop under private ownership. Prices were allowed to fluctuate according to market conditions and wage differentials increased. This policy of economic expediency was, on the whole, successful, and by 1926 industrial production had climbed back to its pre-war level (Lane, 1978, p. 62).

However, there were definite limits to what the NEP could achieve. The main problem for the party leadership was that the mixed economy could not guarantee rapid industrialisation, and it harboured a potentially dangerous contradiction. As long as the agrarian sector was dominated by privately owned smallholdings, it was difficult to extract an economic surplus, let alone increase it. Further, there was a serious risk of breakdown in the fragile worker–peasant alliance. As an urban movement, the Bolsheviks had never had a secure base in the countryside and they were unable to persuade the peasants voluntarily to increase production. Under the Tsarist regime, industrialisation had been financed by the export of grain, which was made possible by investment in agriculture. This solution was not open to the Soviet leaders because they could not afford to become dependent upon unsympathetic foreign regimes. In any case, small peasant proprietors had no incentive to invest in the same way as the pre-1917 landlords and rich peasants. Therefore, a solution to the problem of agricultural production was a precondition for further economic and industrial development. It was found in the policy of forced collectivisation.

The years between 1928 and 1935 saw the further growth of the centralised party-state, now under Stalin, with the twin objectives of rapidly building a heavy industrial base and the swift collectivisation of agriculture to increase production and the surplus available for capital investment. The ambitious policies of the first Five Year Plan (1928–33) could only be achieved by coercion, which is the reason why this period has been likened to the 'Terror' which followed the French Revolution – except that in Russia, it was less arbitrary and more comprehensive.[8] The enforced collectivisation of agriculture completed the party's political control of the rural population, although it did not immediately increase the efficiency of agricultural production. The state's economic objectives were realised by procuring produce at minimum cost from the country-side and selling dear in the towns. At the same time, the trade unions, the collective farm administrations, social services and every other institution were increasingly used as instruments of direct state control for the purposes of fulfilling the economic plan. The human cost in lives and suffering was beyond calculation but the economic results were spectacular. According to a variety of sources, the annual rate of growth in industrial output during the first Five Year Plan was 15 per cent or more; a rate unprecedented in any capitalist country (Lane, 1978, pp. 66–7).

Thus the experience of the Russian revolution and its aftermath shows how a socialist revolutionary movement can itself be transformed in a period of transition. Although the Bolsheviks were successful in consolidating their power, they had to operate in conditions of war, civil conflict and general economic breakdown, none of which were envisaged in Marxist theories. Military survival, the mobilisation of the population and economic growth became goals of overriding importance and they displaced the egalitarian, libertarian and democratic ideals of the revolution into the distant future and into the realms of propaganda.

The foundations for 'socialism in one country' – the Soviet Union – had been firmly established by the Second World War. The countries of Eastern Europe had not yet embarked on a similar route. There had been a working-class revolt in Berlin in 1920 and Hungary had experienced a short-lived Soviet Republic in 1919, but in general the politics of these countries during the inter-war period were dominated by authoritarian conservative or fascist regimes which struggled to fill the vacuum created by the decline of the Hapsburg monarchy and the upheavals of the First World War. It was a period of political instability and economic uncertainty which slowed down the process of industrialisation that commenced in the late nineteenth century. Like Russia before the revolution, industrialisation in Eastern Europe before 1939 was heavily dependent upon foreign capital and expertise. With a high level of state ownership in banking, transport and manufacture, and with a large proportion of foreign ownership in large firms, there was already a high degree of economic centralisation. Industrialisation proceeded from the 'top downwards', leaving the large mass of the population unaffected. In the less industrialised countries such as Hungary and Poland, the industrial working class was less than one-quarter of the total population. Even in Czechoslovakia and Germany – then undivided – both of which had relatively developed industrial sectors, less than 40 per cent of their respective labour forces were employed in mining, manufacturing and construction. The 'transition to socialism' in these countries reflected these broader economic and social circumstances. It was imposed by centralised political and military apparatuses rather than the product of popular, working-class revolution.

After the devastation of the Second World War, during which all the East European countries were under either Nazi occupation or puppet regimes, new conditions and limits for social transformation were set by the presence of Soviet military forces. Although in no country was there an immediate 'communist takeover', the general conditions were ripe for substantial programmes of change, and reforms were launched almost immediately by coalitions of progressive nationalist, social democratic and communist parties.[9] These included land reforms and the nationalisation of key industries.

In each country, there were variations on this common theme. In Poland, immediately after the war, the larger estates were broken up and the land redistributed to peasant smallholders. In Hungary in 1945, the larger estates which accounted for more than one-third of the agricultural land were reallocated to a large number of small farmers. In similar reforms in Czechoslovakia, about one-quarter of farm land was distributed among peasants and former agricultural labourers. By this means, the formerly powerful landowning class was removed and the progressive parties gained a measure of support for their policies among the peasantry.

The second major development in the years immediately following the war was the nationalisation of key industries. In Czechoslovakia, the state took over 60 to 70 per cent of all industrial concerns. In Poland, which more than other Eastern European countries had been been devastated by the war, over 90 per cent of industrial production was in the state sector by 1946 (Lane and Kolankiewicz, 1973, pp. 10–11), while in Hungary 74 per cent of industrial workers had become state employees by 1948. The earliest stage in the transition to socialism in these countries, therefore, was one in which a state-dominated industry coexisted with a predominantly privately owned agricultural sector within a political framework consisting of alliances between nationalist, social democratic and communist groups. The communist parties had to consolidate their power if they were to realise the goals of planning for 'socialist construction'. In practice, this meant pursuing an economic strategy according to the Stalinist model and under Soviet auspices. By 1948–9, the communist parties had achieved supremacy in all the East European states by using a combination of tactics, both democratic and undemocratic.

National differences made for variations in the political methods that were employed. Czechoslovakia, for instance, already had a strong socialist movement – the Communists emerged as the largest single party in the 1946 election – a large working class and practically no aristocracy, and so it was better prepared than other countries for the transition to socialism (Westoby, 1981, pp. 48–51). In other countries, alliances between workers, peasants, intellectuals and the petty bourgeoisie were more unstable. In East Germany, the occupying Soviet military administration ensured that the Communists were the dominant partners in the alliance with the Social Democrats. In all cases, however, it was Stalinist factions within left-wing coalitions which were successful in the struggle for power. They were undoubtedly helped by the continuing presence and potential threat of the Soviet army.

Once in a monopoly or near-monopoly power position, the communist regimes of Eastern Europe were able to develop unhindered towards 'state socialism'. Within only a short period of time, they took further steps towards nationalisation and centralised economic planning. Although privately owned, capitalist forms of production had been inhibited up to 1949, they had not been completely prohibited, so the 'socialist ownership of the means of production' was still incomplete and institutions of economic planning were only beginning to be implemented. The years from 1948 to 1950 witnessed the beginnings of the centrally planned economy along Soviet lines in Eastern Europe. It was known as the 'building of socialist production conditions' as distinct from the formal and legal transfer of factories and land from private to public ownership. State commissions for economic planning set ambitious targets for industrial development and the pace of industrialisation – as measured by investment and output – accelerated rapidly, as did the size of the bureaucratic state apparatus for economic and social control.

The modernisation of agriculture according to socialist principles proved to be a far more demanding task, both economically and politically, just as it had been in Russia in the 1930s. There were several reasons for this. First, ownership of land had been extended in the post-war redistribution with the effect that the average size of farms was considerably reduced. Second, the peasantry's commitment to socialism had been obtained only by the promise of land; there was no indigenous tradition of cooperative or collective methods of production to build upon. Third, agriculture is generally less susceptible to centralised planning than industrial production for reasons of geography, climate and local cultures. In combination, these factors significantly retarded the process of the transition from small-scale peasant farming to 'industrialised' methods of production on large-scale state farms and collectives. In Poland, for instance, where the conditions were perhaps least favourable, only 9 per cent of arable land was collectivised in this early period up to 1956 (Lane and Kolankiewicz, 1973, p. 12) and, partly because the remaining private farms were subject to discrimination and heavy taxation, production actually decreased. This, combined with the decline in workers' living standards because of grandiose Stalinist industrial investment schemes, led to a popular revolt in the industrial city of Poznan in 1956 and the first in a series of economic and political crises in Poland. Similar revolts occurred in other Eastern European countries in the 1950s for largely similar reasons: Czechoslovakia and East Germany in 1953 and, largest of all, Hungary in 1956. These upheavals marked the end of Stalinist industrialisation in its most extreme forms (Stalin had died in 1953) and the beginnings of 'revisionist' alternatives. In those countries where Stalinist policies were pursued most systematically – especially in East Germany, where collectivisation was virtually complete by the end of the 1950s – the peasantry had ceased to exist as a class. But, elsewhere, and particularly in Poland, the peasantry remained a significant force for cultural, religious and economic reasons.

The varieties of state socialism that exist in Eastern Europe today stem from the development strategies adopted by the dictatorial party-state in each country, using the Soviet Union as a general model. Thus there is a common emphasis upon centralised planning for modernisation within the context of an incomplete socialisation of the means of production and unfavourable 'production conditions'; for example, the persistence of 'archaic' or 'bourgeois' institutions inimical to socialist development. Economic strategies vary according to the extent to which private ownership and enterprise is permitted, the degree to which market mechanisms are allowed to determine prices and wages, and the degree of centralisation of economic control. In terms of these criteria, East Germany has advanced farthest along the road to 'socialism', for it has the most collectivised, centralised and developed economy, including a modern, industrially organised agricultural system. Hungary, in contrast, has reached a high level of urban and industrial development by a somewhat different route; the New Economic Mechanism introduced in 1968 allowed for the operation of market mechanisms and a significant degree of decentralisation and depoliticisation of economic planning. Despite these different strategies, the structures of East European societies share a common set of characteristics; they are shaped by one-party, dictatorial states which rule, often coercively, in the name of socialist ideology. The party's key instrument in this process is the state planning apparatus.

The market process or 'exchange system' which is the means of value realisation in capitalism is replaced in state socialism by the central planning system. This may or may not be combined with limited markets as one of the instruments of planning. This use of markets is at a minimum in the Soviet Union and in East Germany where planning is highly centralised but it has played a significant role in Hungary since the New Economic Mechanism was established. In each case, however, investment decisions are guided by the centrally established goals which include economic growth, a strong and balanced economy and socialist construction, rather than by the criterion of profit for individual capitalists. Where market forces are allowed a measure of free play, it is almost invariably in such 'secondary' areas as consumer product pricing rather than in the differentiation of wages or the prices of raw materials.

Although there is considerable variation between countries in their economic planning institutions, they always closely interlock with the political institutions of the one-party state. At the summit, the key structural decisions are taken by the supreme political authority, the Politburo, which sets targets for economic growth, the priorities for different industries and so on. These general targets are elaborated in the form of detailed plans – Annual Plans or Five Year Plans – which identify areas for investment, define prices, set output targets and specify rates of growth for industrial sectors and products. In the Soviet Union, coordination of the planning functions of the various ministries is performed by *Gosplan*, the

All-Union State Planning Committee and its regional subsidiaries. Planning decisions are then executed by state appointees of state monopoly enterprises. This is a 'command' system which enables key economic decisions to be taken centrally. However, that does not mean that every single facet of economic life is directly controlled by state planning agencies. Even if it were desirable from the point of view of a command economy, the administrative apparatus cannot plan for every detail of labour allocation or the distribution of consumer goods.

In Poland, privately owned peasant agriculture is tolerated within the framework of central state planning and the same is true of small-scale enterprises in Hungary. Even in the Soviet Union – particularly since the fall of Khrushchev in 1965 – some use of market mechanisms is seen as an appropriate adjunct to the central plan, especially in the attempt to match the output of consumer goods with consumer demand. This trend is likely to continue as the industrial system becomes more complex, simply because a vastly greater number of economic variables will need to be taken into account in the planning process. The limits of planning may also be seen in determining the level of wages; rates are fixed at the centre, but bonus systems operate according to local variations in the performance of enterprises. Similarly, efficient enterprises which have a surplus after meeting their costs, including the fixed surplus payable to the state, may retain a proportion of this for the direct benefit of employees. This may be used in the form of extra earnings, social services or capital investment at the discretion of enterprises. In Soviet agriculture, although the command principle applies directly to collective and state farms, there exists alongside these a large private sector, with an average of 1½ acres per household (Lane, 1978, p. 286). This generates agricultural output which is sold alongside collective farm produce in urban markets. In addition to these examples of legitimate markets operating within the planned system, there are numerous unofficial and illegal markets in goods and services which fill the gaps created by inefficiencies in the state planning system or meet consumer demands which cannot be fulfilled by legal means – for example, foreign clothes or currency.

By comparison with the Western capitalist societies, the state socialist countries of East Europe have a record of rapid capital accumulation, especially in their early years. There are several reasons for this. First, with the exception of Czechoslovakia and East Germany, they inherited relatively low levels of industrialisation and much of the industrial infrastructure which did exist was devastated in the Second World War. Second, the threat of external intervention in Russia after 1917 and during the 'cold war' period after 1948 provided a strong incentive for rapid industrialisation to achieve both economic and military strength. Third, the highly centralised planning mechanisms, which were adopted in all the East European countries in the Stalinist period of the 1950s and into the 1960s, gave priority to investment and capital accumulation. The result was that only a small proportion of the economic surplus was used to improve the living standards of productive workers.

The scale and speed of industrialisation is illustrated by the following figures. In East Germany, annual growth rates in the 1950s were between 5 and 10 per cent and they averaged 4.5 per cent in the 1960s (Zauberman, 1964, p. 107). In the Soviet Union, the gross national product rose at an average rate of 5.8 per cent each year between 1951 and 1955 (Lane, 1978, p. 287). In all the state socialist countries, rates of increase have tended to slow down in more recent years. The distribution of the economic surplus – and the priority given to capital investment – is well illustrated by the case of Czechoslovakia which, between 1948 and 1953, had a similar rate of growth to East Germany and the Soviet Union while average real wages *declined* by about 10 per cent during the same period (Zauberman, 1964, p. 95). Although it is true that the planned economies experienced considerable fluctuations, some of which reached crisis proportions, it was not until the 1970s that they showed signs of stagnation similar to those in the West. But at the crucial stage of political and economic consolidation, the regimes in the different East European countries were able to achieve fast rates of growth, although largely at the expense of personal consumption.

How long can rapid growth be sustained by these priorities before low living standards generate serious social discontent? Certainly not indefinitely. State socialism was, and continues to be, sustained by a combination of consent, coercion and ideology. Consent has been regularly reinforced by periods of 'reform', socialist ideology has been 'adapted' to national circumstances, and methods of coercion by the military or by state police have been applied when other methods have failed. This is the background against which it is necessary to understand the apparent contradictions of state socialism; for instance, the combination of egalitarian principles with unusually rigid, hierarchical institutions, and the socialisation of the productive forces but with an absence of democratic control. Thus state socialism is far from being a unitary, 'totalitarian' system in which every individual and social relationship is permanently dominated by centralised state planning.[10] In other words, it is a system which operates a socialist model of society – or, strictly speaking, a model of the *transition* to socialism – with highly centralised and politicised bureaucratic institutions. In turn, these generate new social inequalities as well as eradicating some of those which are endemic to capitalism and previous modes of production.

What, then, are the core features of East European state socialism? The task of identifying these is facilitated by their close dependence on the Soviet model and their common experience in the aftermath of the Second World War. In addition, they participate in supranational structures – Comecon and the Warsaw Pact – which integrate them economically, politically and militarily to a greater extent than most of the countries of the capitalist 'Western alliance'. In considering the core features of state socialism as a structured system of social relations, it is convenient to distinguish between their 'primary' and 'secondary' characteristics. The primary characteristics may be described as follows:

1   The basic means of production are state-owned and controlled, by a centralised plan. The socialisation of the means of production is not necessarily complete but the 'commanding heights' of banking, industry and the infrastructure of services are invariably in state hands. Even when there remains extensive private ownership of land, production is still normally directed by the state.

2   There is a substantial bureaucratic state apparatus which implements economic and social plans according to principles laid down by the party.

3   Political rule is by a hierarchically organised single party which controls the bureaucracy, the police and military forces. Typically, there are parallel party and administrative

institutions at each level from national and regional government down to factories.

4   The legitimating ideology is socialist; that is, it claims direct descent from Marx and Lenin, usually in combination with various indigenous socialist traditions.

These features are found in all the state socialist societies of East Europe and the Soviet Union. It is the close interrelationship between the economic, political and administrative spheres within state socialism which clearly differentiates it from capitalism, even though the latter in its monopoly phase shows signs of moving in this direction. Some commentators have mistakenly interpreted this as a sign of 'convergence' between the two systems.[11] Their mistake is to emphasise one of the primary characteristics at the expense of others – for example, growing state intervention in economic planning in Western countries – when the essential character of state socialism lies in its combination of all the four above-mentioned features.

The secondary characteristics show greater variation between countries although they tend to follow from the primary features. In the first place, there is a strong bias towards capital accumulation, even at the expense of the population as consumers. The historical necessity of building 'socialism in one country' helps to account for this, but the dictatorial party-state following a materialist ideology seems regularly to subordinate individual 'needs' to collective 'needs', whereas the reverse has been generally true in capitalist societies. Second, as a consequence of the central planning system, there is a tendency for quantifiable economic goals to be given priority over non-quantifiable social aims; a tendency which is reinforced by the official information media. Third, the close relationship of the economy to the party-state system makes it particularly vulnerable to arbitrary changes of policy. Finally, the 'official' status of socialist ideology has encouraged a degree of uniformity in culture, education and the sciences which is far greater than in the liberal pluralist cultures of the Western capitalist countries.

It is evident that the structures of state socialism generate economic and social inequalities despite their egalitarian ideology. The nature of these inequalities is a key question. Do social classes exist under state socialism or has the socialisation of the means of production abolished them? Some observers (Cliff, 1974; Harman, 1983) have argued that similarities in the mode of capital accumulation between East and West are strong enough to justify calling the East European societies 'state capitalist'. Another question concerns the new inequalities which are generated by the bureaucratic party-state and the possibility that these may be transmitted between generations, even without the mechanisms of private accumulation and inheritance. These problems are the subject of the next chapter.

5

State Socialism, Class and Inequality

According to the official ideology of state socialism, the abolition of private ownership of the means of production creates the conditions for a society without classes and class conflict. Since those who contribute to the productive process are also 'owners', they have an equal entitlement to its rewards, so they cannot be exploited. In this chapter we examine the key assumption behind this claim: the supposed harmony of interests within socialist production relations. Further, we consider whether significant new types of alienation, inequality and social conflict may be generated by state socialism.

The analysis of the productive process within East European societies must begin by specifying the social relations of production. Within capitalism, these relationships are characterised by a fundamental distinction between the functions of capital (ownership, coordination and control) and the functions of labour (direct and indirect production of the economic surplus). In the case of state socialism, where ownership of the means of production is predominantly collectivised, the basic distinction between privately owned capital and labour is no longer fundamental to the structure of social relationships. However, some aspects of the productive process continue to share great similarities. Labour, of course, is necessary for the creation of the economic surplus under socialism as it is under capitalism. Further, both are complex industrial systems requiring a range of ancillary tasks which are not directly productive. Likewise, the task of coordinating a productive process which has a complex division of labour is common to both socialism and capitalism. The fundamental difference between the two social systems, as far as the relations of production are concerned, is in the nature of ownership and control.

Under capitalism, private ownership of the means of production gives corporate management the right to direct and control the activities of workers and to appropriate the economic surplus product which they produce. What happens to these rights in a state socialist country? First, ownership is legally transferred to government ministries which are accountable to the political institutions of the society – for example, elected deputies, the Supreme Soviet, and so on. Second, the right to control the productive process is vested in enterprise directors who are appointed by government ministries. Compared with the directors and managers of capitalist corporations who pursue profit by whatever means available and in competition with others, the directors of state socialist enterprises have less freedom for manoeuvre; they are subordinated to economic plans devised by ministries. The role of state planning, is, therefore, fundamental; it determines the processes whereby the economic surplus is produced and appropriated. The distribution of this 'publicly owned' surplus is subject to claims by all sectors of society and is, accordingly, a deliberate *political* process.

Production relations under state socialism may be schematically depicted as in figure 3, using analogous categories to those in chapter 2. In place of the 'functions of capital', there is the 'state planning' function, performed by government ministries and executed by enterprise directors. The most significant division continues to be between those who perform the functions of labour on the one hand and those whose tasks are concerned with planning and coordination on the other. Thus, under the state planning function, there are two major tasks: (1) central planning, including research and development; and (2) control and coordination. The functions of labour are (3) the execution of necessary but non-productive tasks, and (4) the production of the economic surplus. Under state socialism these functions correspond closely with those under capitalism and this is reflected in the similarities between capitalist and socialist work relationships and processes. There are also some superficial similarities between the functions of capital and the functions of state planning; for instance, managers supervise and coordinate the productive process using similar techniques, but

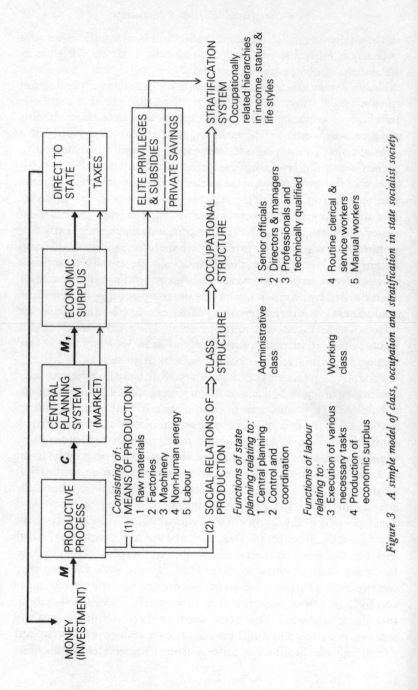

Figure 3 *A simple model of class, occupation and stratification in state socialist society*

while under capitalism the economic surplus takes the form of private profit, under socialism it has the form of politically accountable funds which are then available for fulfilling various social needs. Although some of these funds are actually disbursed in the form of subsidies to the political elite, the social relations of production, in this simplified model, do not contain the same potential for social antagonism as they do under capitalism.

While some allowance must be made for variations between state socialist countries, especially according to their degree of centralisation, there is sufficient similarity of purpose in the functions of state planning in all these countries to warrant treating them together. In our simple model, we emphasise central planning, although this never exists in a perfect form.[1] The more complex the system of production, the more likely it is that tasks will be delegated and decentralised, with a greater reliance upon market mechanisms.

The overall direction of the accumulation process in state socialist societies is determined by the ministries which, in turn, are accountable to the party elite.[2] The ministries themselves are coordinated by state committees which are responsible for such matters as economic planning, science and technology, and investment. In the Soviet Union, these include *Gosplan* (in charge of economic planning as a whole), *Gostsen* (responsible for prices) and *Stroibank* (the investment credit bank). The ministries are responsible for the administration of the various branches of the economy according to the guidelines of the central plan. Like the economic ministries of the Western capitalist countries, they attempt to regulate and control the pattern of economic activity, but, unlike them, they are political bodies with far more extensive powers. The function of central planning is fundamentally different from the strategies of individual capitalists and corporations in the West. State plans set short- and medium-range goals which, although expressed in economic terms – for example, growth rates for industrial output, provision of services and so on – are the translation of politically defined objectives. Thus decisions about capital construction, the use of new technologies or the diversification of products are made not primarily according to calculations about their potential profitability, market impact or competitiveness, but in terms of whether they will contribute to party-determined goals – in short, to the 'construction of socialism'. Of course, profit-and-loss accounting is used to monitor the performance of enterprises on a day-to-day basis, but of the three essential elements of industrial capitalism – production for profit, the factory system and the market for commodities – only one (the factory system) is present in state socialism. Profit, then, is replaced by a state-acquired economic surplus and the market is replaced by the state monopoly of production, distribution and exchange.

Between the central planning institutions and the individual enterprise there are 'associations', which consist of either vertically or horizontally integrated groupings of enterprises. These have been created since the 1960s as a response to the increasing scale and complexity of economic organisation. They are involved in the administration of the productive process rather than in production itself. For example, the task of the Soviet 'industrial associations' and their counterparts in East Germany – the 'associations of nationalised industries' – is to foster cooperation between enterprises, to elaborate the details of the Plan, to raise the quality of goods and to improve working conditions. They are also responsible for the training of managers. Not least, they are required to develop 'socialist competition'. It is clear that many of these functions correspond quite closely to the functions of coordination in the West which are met either within capitalist corporations by the upper levels of management or by inter-industry groupings, for example trade associations and cartels.

The productive process is controlled by enterprise directors whose objectives are to fulfil, or if possible overfulfil, the state plan. Managerial authority is vested in directors within hierarchical organisational structures. This, together with the fact that the performance of these enterprises is measured by profit-and-loss accounting, can give the impression that enterprise directors are in a very similar position to general managers in capitalist corporations. However, in the Soviet case at least, the factory administration with the director at its head is only one of *three* institutions which constitute the enterprise as a social entity (Lane and O'Dell, 1978, pp. 22ff.). The Communist Party exercises a distinctive control function through its representatives. Further, there is invariably a trade union branch which serves as an important mechanism for integrating workers through the sponsorship of social and welfare activities. Thus neither the party nor the trade union in the Soviet factory has a direct parallel in the West. Trade unions do not play an oppositional role because the interests of those who fulfil the functions of the central plan *and* those who fulfil the functions of labour are officially seen to be convergent, if not identical. Consequently, the party's control function is to assert the interests of 'society' – which is understood according to the principles of socialist development – against the possibly divergent interests of professional and technically more specialised management. Hence, the party ratifies appointments and promotes activities which contribute to the social as well as the economic development of the enterprise.

The functions of labour within the state socialist productive system are expressed in the activities of direct producers and those who contribute indirectly to the production of the economic surplus. They occupy the same subordinate position as labour within the relations of production of capitalist society. It is the same process of converting raw materials and other items into goods for distribution and consumption which creates the economic surplus. Under capitalism, those who perform the function of labour are denied the total amount of the value of the commodities they produce. In a state socialist society, the general level of wages is determined by the state planning process but it is also less than the total value of what workers produce. However, whilst under capitalism the surplus is at the disposal of private owners and corporate shareholders, in state socialism the surplus is available to the central planners to meet social needs as defined by the party. In other words, there is a fundamental difference in who owns and controls the economic surplus.

In many other respects, the function of labour in state socialism and capitalism is similar. In mines, farms and factories and other sites of production, workers are wage-labourers. Their work is increasingly characterised by the application of machinery, the detailed division of labour and 'alienation' from the processes of planning, distribution and exchange of the goods they produce.[3] To a large extent, the processes of technical innovation, occupational specialisation and work organisation are parallel with those in the monopoly stage of capitalism. Although the motive is not the pursuit of private profit, the criteria of efficiency and productivity are still used to gauge economic success.

However, there are some significant differences in the function of labour under capitalism and state socialism. The first is a consequence of the more recent industrialistion of most East European societies. This means that by comparison with many capitalist countries, a higher proportion of the labour force is still directly engaged in agricultural production. There is also the fact that technology tends to be applied in ways which are labour-using rather than labour-saving. Second, there is an ideological difference. The official view in state socialist societies is that industrial workers are, politically speaking, the vanguard of society. Third, there is no 'free market' for labour; instead, the state attempts to allocate labour according to the needs of the Plan. This is done by such methods as directing graduates to their first jobs and manipulating wage rates and bonuses. This means that, in theory at least, unemployment is eliminated except where the system of 'directed' labour breaks down. In short, then, the function of labour under state socialism is less vulnerable to market fluctuations and more systematically integrated into the productive system than under capitalism. This is reflected in the character of social class relations in state socialism which are sometimes officially described as 'non-antagonistic' and which are certainly different in character from those in capitalist societies.

To refer to the social relations of production within state socialist societies as 'non-antagonistic' is to distinguish them from the relations of production in a capitalist society.[4] We described the latter as antagonistic because the process of extracting the economic surplus is a process of expropriation by individuals and groups for private use. Antagonism, which Marx and Engels likened to 'a more or less veiled civil war' (1969, p. 93), is endemic to this arrangement, whether or not feelings of resentment are immediately apparent among workers. The socialisation of the productive process removes the objective basis of this antagonism by transposing the economic conflict over the surplus into the political sphere. It creates a structure of relations which are differentiated by their functions so that in place of civil war there is a more or less peaceful alliance. Nevertheless, these functional differences can be, and in practice are, the bases for inequalities in power, privilege and prestige.

So it is still appropriate to describe the social groupings, based respectively on the functions of state planning and the functions of labour, as social classes. This is because the differentiation of functions within state socialist relations of production shapes the entire system of social relations, political power and status. This has led some writers to view the Soviet Union and East European countries as variations of capitalism – as 'state capitalist' societies – in which those responsible for state planning are directly comparable to the bourgeoisie in Western capitalism.[5] This, however, ignores both differences in ownership and the direction and purpose of the accumulation process, which in state socialism is determined politically through priorities as set by the state Plan. Others, especially Soviet writers in the 1930s, depicted the society emerging from the civil war and rapid industrialisation as one without antagonistic classes and characterised by social harmony. Neither of these views does justice to the complexities of social relations in Soviet and Eastern European countries. Our use of the term 'state socialism', and our insistence that the term 'socialism' must be qualified by reference to the form of the state, express the belief that these countries represent an alternative path of development to the pure forms of both capitalism and socialism. In different ways, the use of the terms 'state capitalist' and 'socialist' reflect a selective use of the evidence – either an over-emphasis upon quasi-capitalist features or too much stress on socialist theory rather than practice.

In fact, differentiation in the relations of production is the condition for the existence of social classes. Antagonism does not follow in every mode of production from differentiation *per se*; it occurs in capitalism because of the exploitative nature of the productive process. In state socialism, however, the objective conditions for non-exploitative relations are met, although political opposition and acute social conflicts may emerge over the direction of the planning process, the distribution of the economic surplus and the exercise of state and enterprise control systems. Other conflicts occur because capitalist social forms continue to persist within state socialism; for example, small-scale private ownership and the application of Western-based management theory. However, these destabilising aspects of state socialist class relations can be described as 'non-antagonistic' because they can be resolved, in principle at least, by adjustments and changes within the state socialist system. In contrast, the antagonistic contradictions of capital–labour relations within capitalism have tended to undermine the legitimacy and stability of the system as a whole. The implications of this analysis will be explored more fully in chapters 7 and 8 on crisis tendencies.

One of the obstacles to understanding the class structures of capitalism and state socialism is the common tendency to compare them using different criteria. For instance, Western critics of the Soviet system often interpret the evidence of conformity, stability and lack of conflict as a product of a system of repression which sets too high a price on protest. But analogous evidence in capitalist countries is read as a sign of approval and support. The position adopted here is derived from analytical categories which are equally applicable to both sides and do not depend on such 'comparisons'. It is not intended to play down the role of conflict but rather to highlight the nature of its social origins within each system. The potential for conflict, even within the 'non-antagonistic' class relations of state socialism, is considerable and is one of the important themes of chapter 8.

In our simplified model of state socialist society, the functions of state planning are performed by an administrative class and the functions of labour by the working class. This is a statement of objective class position within the state socialist productive system; that is, 'class in itself'. There are, however, a number of problems in any class analysis of state socialist countries. For example, how are the relationships between the administrative and working class expressed in patterns of economic and social inequality? What is the evidence of class awareness? What is the pattern of social mobility between classes? Further, are there social categories which are marginal or excluded from the main class groupings? These are central issues in any analysis of state socialist societies but, unfortunately, they are difficult to explore because of the paucity of reliable comparative data.

Class relations are rarely visible. Normally they are expressed through divisions within the occupational structure. While this is true of both state socialism and capitalism, there are certain significant differences between their occupational profiles. The five categories which we used to describe the capitalist occupational structure in chapter 2 are not fully applicable to state socialism. It is highest-level occupations contributing either to state planning or to private capital accumulation which provide the greatest contrast between the two social systems. In the following occupational categories, the first two are peculiar to state-owned enterprises. The third has similarities with technically and professionally qualified groups in capitalist societies, and the fourth and fifth have quite close counterparts among the clerical, service and manual groups within capitalist occupational structures.

1 Senior state officials.
2 Directors and managers of state enterprises and bureaucracies.
3 Professional and technically qualified workers.
4 Routine non-manual, clerical and manual service workers.
5 Semi- and unskilled manual workers.

Senior state officials, directors and managers fulfil different functions in state socialist and capitalist societies. Although the managing director of a capitalist firm and the director of a state enterprise may perform a number of very similar tasks and may even enjoy similar financial and social privileges, their respective positions within the hierarchies of capitalist and state socialist society are different. The state socialist enterprise director is subject to the dictates of the Plan, has less personal autonomy and responsibility, and is subject to more political control. It follows that the privileges and fringe benefits which officials and senior managers enjoy depend on continuing political approval, not upon personal or corporate economic power.

One of the prominent features of state socialism is the persistence of income inequalities: the realisation of the socialist ideal of income based on 'need' is still a very long way off. There was a fundamental reduction in inequalities in the aftermath of the October revolution in the Soviet Union and, to a lesser extent, in East Europe after the Second World War, when the means for the accumulation of private wealth were abolished. Today, however, 'socialist' egalitarian principles are expressed not so much in attempts to achieve absolute equality as in distinctions based on such criteria as 'the degree of complexity of labour', 'efficiency' and the quantity and quality of 'work performed'.

It is difficult to obtain reliable data on income inequalities in state socialist countries. Neither the Soviet Union nor the other East European countries publish data on national income distribution. Some information is available, however, on average earnings for different categories of workers. Leaving aside for the moment the question of the political elite, there are two striking results when the pay structures of similar occupations in capitalist and state socialist societies are compared. The first is the general similarity in these structures. Although the dispersion about the average is somewhat lower within state socialism, this is mainly because the highest level of earnings, for example of directors and senior managers, is lower; among the broad range of occupations with average or below average incomes, there is close similarity. The second feature is that the relative earnings of routine non-manual, clerical and service workers are significantly lower than in most capitalist countries. These points are illustrated in table 6 which shows the pay structure in the engineering industry in several countries.

As far as the overall range of inequality is concerned, the data show significantly narrower differentials than are found in most Western capitalist countries. This is reinforced by the absence of unearned income (for example, dividends, interest on invested capital, etc.) of the kind which is enjoyed by privileged groups in the West. Of course, we should not ignore the considerable fringe benefits which members of the administrative class enjoy in the Soviet Union and East Europe (Matthews, 1978), but even so there is no doubt that state socialism has redistributed incomes to a far greater degree than any capitalist society, including the social democracies. To the extent that the mechanisms of private capital accumulation and the inheritance of wealth have been abolished within state socialism, economic inequalities of the scale found in capitalist societies are unlikely to reappear. However, income and goods will continue to be unevenly distributed in state socialist countries according to differences of economic function, power and prestige.

The ranking of occupations according to income in table 6 represents a hierarchy of skills and roles within the production process. Overall, the evidence suggests a division according to educational qualifications and levels of responsibility; that is, between those occupations which execute state plans and those which perform the tasks of labour. Thus we can see a close parallel with capitalist societies where the pattern of life-time earnings does not consist of a smoothly graded series of steps, but contains a

TABLE 6 PAY STRUCTURE IN ENGINEERING INDUSTRIES IN SELECTED EAST EUROPEAN COUNTRIES AND THE UK

	Czechoslovakia 1962	East Germany 1962	Poland 1962	USSR[a] 1970	UK[b] 1970
Management (factory directors)	188	160	166	144	254 General Manager 208 Works Manager of several works
Non-manual workers in highly qualified technical–scientific jobs	151	131	142	99	117
Qualified non-manual workers, including technicians	58	72	93	97	103
Highly qualified workers in jobs with mental and manual functions (tool setters)	60	54	70	106	100
Skilled manual workers (fitters, welders)	–	–	–	104	103
Semi-skilled manual workers	–	–	–	106	89
Non-manual workers with medium qualifications	–	–	–	67	83
Unskilled manual workers	–	–	–	79	76

[a] Figures based on average monthly earnings in Leningrad.
[b] Figures based on average weekly earnings in UK.
Maximum salary rates of occupations in four state socialist countries compared with average pay in similar occupations in the UK. Figures expressed as relatives to the unweighted mean of 8 occupational grades = 100.
Sources: Lane, 1982, p. 48; Phelps Brown, 1977, pp. 40-1

significant cleavage between 'middle'- and 'working'-class occupations. There is, however, a significant difference in the relative position of the lower-income groups. Skilled manual workers generally receive higher incomes than qualified non-manual workers. This is unusual in capitalist countries, especially when 'life-time earnings' are taken into account. In view of the fact that in Soviet-type economies wages rates are practically the only means of influencing labour productivity and attracting labour to new branches of industry, it may be that this 'inverted' pattern of occupational earnings is a necessary substitute for the market mechanism and unemployment. Although the while-collar/blue-collar distinction is not reflected in income differentials, it may still be relevant for status; there are descriptive evidence and survey data to suggest that routine manual work is no more appealing or prestigious in state socialist countries than in the west (Haraszti, 1977; Connor, 1979).

In contrast with capitalist societies, the occupational contours of state socialist countries are not shaped directly by markets for labour. Market mechanisms – which are highly imperfect even in capitalist societies – are replaced by planning mechanisms. The most important of these is the fixing of wage-rates. These are not at the discretion of individual enterprises but are set by the Plan, which allows for variations in the supply of labour as well as for differences in education, skill and productivity. The labour-planning process may be more or less directive depending on the country. Planning in the Soviet Union, for example, has entailed the 'organised recruitment' of labour. This has sometimes meant the forced relocation of workers, and at other times the use of financial inducements. In the early 1930s, the primary objective was to meet the demand for labour in the rapidly growing industrial sector by importing workers from the countryside to the cities. In the period since the war, there has been greater emphasis on the need to attract workers to the 'frontier areas' of Siberia and Central Asia. According to some sources, more than two-thirds of all manual workers in the Soviet Union are on piece-rates, a classic device to stimulate output which can be adapted to influence the allocation of labour.

The system of labour recruitment and allocation in state socialist societies is subject to a number of influences which are resistant to 'socialist planning' and which generate divisions with the occupational structure. Some of these are not unlike the divisions which exist within capitalism as a consequence of labour market processes and they persist in state socialism in spite of the socialist egalitarian ideology. There are three main sources of division which have significance for occupational earnings, status and mobility. These are, in turn, the pattern of urban development, ethnicity and gender. The first is explained by the persistence of traditional agriculture. For example, in the Soviet Union and Poland, the agricultural population in 1979 was 17 and 31 per cent of the total respectively. This reflects both the relatively recent development of industry and the low productivity of agriculture. In East Germany, where agriculture is both more capital-intensive and more collectivised than in other state socialist societies, the rural population is 10 per cent of this total, which is still larger than in the capitalist countries of Europe and North America. Although both agriculture and industry are vital to the production of the economic surplus, there is a considerable difference in the level of earnings between the two sectors. In the Soviet Union, for example, average monthly earnings in the agricultural sector in 1980 were 149.2 roubles compared with 179.2 for the manufacturing sector (International Labour Office, 1982). This inequality of incomes is reflected in the general position of the Soviet peasantry, which is still closer to traditional farming methods and rural values than to the socialist ideal of highly industrialised, collective production.

The second division is also related to the pattern of economic development. The Soviet population is made up of numerous Russian and non-Russian groups and the uneven development of the productive forces often accentuates ethnic divisions. Although official policy advocates the development of regions and the integration of all ethnic groups into a single socialist society, the reality is different. While there has been some levelling of geographical differences, this has been concentrated in the Russian homeland, so that regional differences – using a variety of economic and social indicators, including income – leave many non-Russian territories and ethnic groups at a relative disadvantage. Being smaller in scale than the Soviet Union, most East European countries are more ethnically homogeneous and regional differences are less pronounced.

Third, there are gender divisions within the occupational structure. In capitalist societies, where market mechanisms encourage dualistic or segmented patterns in the division of labour, one of the most important boundaries is between 'women's work' and 'men's work'. In state socialism, the principle of equality has been applied to gender relationship and economic planning has encouraged a high level of participation by women in the labour force and a certain amount of desegregation of occupations, especially in the professions and in the provision of various 'para-domestic' amenities like creches and canteens at the workplace. However, this process is far from complete: average earnings for women are rarely more than two-thirds of the average for men, women are concentrated in low-wage, unskilled occupations such as clothing manufacture (McAuley, 1981). The persistence of a strong male ideological bias is best seen in the fact that women still perform the overwhelming majority of domestic labour, even when they have jobs outside the home. Thus the evidence concerning occupational structures in East European societies indicates that while state socialist planning can, in theory, replace the labour market with more rational and egalitarian means of employment allocation, it is in practice strongly inhibited by a historical and ideological legacy of pre-industrial and patriarchal forms.

The general pattern of social stratification in state socialist societies resulting from this mixture of relatively recent economic development, state ownership of the means of production and systematic central planning has had a number of distinctive effects which are not evident in Western capitalist countries. The basic inequalities in income and status, which have some similarities in all countries East and West, are permeated with political significance in state socialist societies. The summit of the occupational and social hierarchy is, in fact, a small political elite, perhaps only 2 or 3 per cent of the total working population, which is completely identified with the upper ranks of the Communist Party or its equivalent. It is essentially a political grouping which consists of the chief functionaries of the state and its planning institutions. Although membership of the Communist Party does not guarantee a position in the elite, the party is nevertheless the key mechanism for upward social mobility. The routes via education, professional careers and private accumulation of wealth which exist in capitalism are either not available or require political endorsement in state socialism. *Apparatchik*, a Russian term to describe those who have influence within the state bureaucracy, is appropriate because it expresses their access to privileges by virtue of their official functions rather than through private ownership of wealth or property. These may be acquired by various legitimate or illegitimate means, but personal fortunes cannot be the basis for the elite's authority in state socialist countries.

The elite tends to be highly cohesive because there is no institutional separation between the economic and political spheres. Whereas in capitalist countries, there may be conflicts of interests between dominant economic, political and cultural groups, serious ruptures are largely avoided in the more closely integrated state socialist systems, where the party has control of key positions in each of these spheres. It is this which has guaranteed the party a level of political and social control which has only been matched by fascist regimes in Western capitalist countries. This leads some commentators to describe the system of state socialism as 'totalitarian' *per se*, but such an explanation exaggerates the comprehensiveness of social and political control.[6] In fact, there are many divergent interests between, for example, economic, industrial, military and political leaders but the means for resolving these exist within the party machinery and they are normally well hidden from public view. Whereas in capitalist countries, elites are perpetuated through mechanisms of inheritance and exclusive education, the relatively recent origins of state socialism in the Soviet Union and in East Europe means that many members of the elite are only one or two generations removed from peasant or manual working-class backgrounds.

In terms of life chances and life styles, there is a distinct stratum formed out of groups whose function is essentially to administer various aspects of the Plan. 'Intelligentsia' is the term commonly used throughout East Europe and the Soviet Union to describe those engaged in such activities, which includes a substantial cultural, scientific or intellectual component. It comprises 'specialists', administrators, technicians, teachers, cultural workers and others with higher educational qualifications. They are distinct from the elite in two main ways. First, they are not functionaries of the state in a direct sense; they do not work for the central and local organisations of the party and government but within educational, media and various professional bodies. Second, they have a much larger and more diverse cluster of occupations. Although they have expanded rapidly under state socialism because of the need for professional expertise in economic and social planning, they have retained a measure of autonomy from the state. This is partly because of the intellectual and cultural legacy of pre-revolutionary central Europe and partly because of the quasi-independent structures of scientific knowledge, professional training and organisation. This gives the intelligentsia an important position in the stratification system of state socialist society (Konrad and Szelenyi, 1979).

In theory, if not always in practice, the intelligentsia is charged by the state to develop the scientific, productive and creative forces necessary for the 'construction of socialism'. However, the priorities of many of the intelligentsia may diverge from those of the elite, which is committed first and foremost to the existing bureaucratic command system rather than to its development and change. Hence, there is the widespread phenomenon of intellectual dissidence. The intelligentsia's autonomy from the state, nevertheless, is constrained by its role in the productive process and within the occupational structure. In fact, there is probably a greater tendency for the interests of the elite and the intelligentsia to converge rather than to diverge. There is, in any case, some overlap between the two strata; for example, the Soviet Academy of Sciences is, by definition, an elite institution but, at the same time, it is a focus for the activities of the intelligentsia as a whole.

Manual and non-manual workers comprise the largest stratum in state socialist society. Clerical and unqualified and junior 'white-collar' workers are different from the intelligentsia in two main respects: they have less education and less autonomy. But, as in capitalist societies, there is a qualitative and socially significant difference between manual and non-manual workers. Although this is not reflected in relative earnings – in fact, manual earnings in basic industries are often higher than white-collar earnings – non-manual employees tend to have a higher level of education and are more likely to be party members. This difference between the two categories is also reflected in friendship patterns and life styles. The functional importance of productive work and its contribution to society is more generally acknowledged in state socialist than in capitalist countries. The higher status of manual workers in the former is the one major difference between the hierarchies of occupational prestige in the two systems and would seem to be partly a function of socialist ideology, although this may be of diminishing importance as revolutionary ideals fade. Further, there is evidence that manual workers in state socialist countries are more tightly integrated into the social order (Lane and O'Dell, 1978, p. 51). This is because the mechanisms of social integration are more comprehensive as a result of the fusion of industrial, political and welfare institutions. The economic enterprise integrates all these aspects in a comprehensive manner and, as such, it is a key element in a wider process of social control.

Finally, the peasantry remains an important stratum, although it is a residual one within the long-term development of state socialism. The boundary between peasants and workers is of great social significance in those countries where there is still a numerically large agricultural population, especially in Poland and the Soviet Union. Although the peasantry occupies an inferior position in the hierarchies of income, power and social prestige, it is distinctive in its attachment to private property and traditional values, including religion. It also expresses the fundamental differences that remain between rural and urban ways of life. Compared with the advanced capitalist societies where farming is highly mechanised, agricultural methods in Poland and the Soviet Union are largely geared to peasants' immediate needs, with production for surplus having a lower priority. Strictly speaking, collective farmers and agricultural workers on state farms are not peasants, since they neither own land nor decide what should be produced. But in other respects the nature of their work, attitudes and life styles have many of the characteristics of the traditional peasantry. The economic, social and political significance of the agricultural population can, therefore, be seen in several ways. Economically, it constitutes a large reserve of unskilled labour which has often been mobilised for rapid industrialisation. At the same time, it has resisted state attempts to mechanise, to modernise and to increase agricultural production. Politically, the worker–peasant alliance which was so indispensable in the Soviet revolution is still necessary, if only because the state recognises that agricultural production is central to its programme for industrial development. In the case of Poland, in particular, where Catholicism has deep roots in the countryside, the peasantry (or agricultural stratum) exists as an impediment to rapid social and economic change.

Our analysis of class and inequality in state socialist societies leads to three major conclusions. First, classes exist because there are relations of production which give rise to functional specialisations between major social groupings. Thus, at the most general level, we can make a distinction between an 'administrative' and a 'working' class. However, they are not diametrically opposed like the bourgeoisie and proletariat in capitalist society. Within the admittedly narrow perspective of the economic Plan, the relationship may be described as non-antagonistic. Second, economic inequalities are not the outcome of conflict over a privately appropriated surplus but are determined by a central planning process which decides the distribution of rewards according to criteria of skill, qualification and functional contribution. Having said that, it is important to emphasise that the range of inequality in East European societies is far smaller than in Western capitalist countries. Finally, the political elite, with its many privileges, some of which can be passed on to the next generation, is hardly in a position to become a self-sustaining and closed social group if only because it has no legal claim to ownership of the means of production. Having thus far focused upon a number of common features of East European countries in this chapter, we now turn our attention to some of the more important differences that exist between state socialist societies.

6

Contrasts in State Socialism: National Differences

The overwhelming importance of the Soviet Union as an economic and political power in Eastern Europe makes it quite legitimate to speak in general terms of 'Soviet-type' societies. There exists a pattern of economic and social development, essentially Stalinist in origin, which has shaped the social structures of all the East European countries. But neither the historical precedence of the Soviet Union as a prototype nor its political and military grip on the other state socialist countries is the guarantee of a singular path of development in the future. While there is greater uniformity among these countries than among the Western capitalist societies, there are, nevertheless, significant differences between them. These contrasts, together with their accompanying political tensions, are important for understanding the dynamic and direction of change in Eastern Europe.

In broad terms, the variations stem from three sources. First, each state socialist country occupies a different position on the historical trajectory of industrial development; for example, in the relative size of its agricultural population or the level of industrial output. In Eastern Europe, the differences are at least as great, if not greater, in this respect than in the countries of Western Europe. The level of industrial development has, in turn, shaped the specific policies of socialisation and central planning. Second, there is growing diversity in economic planning strategies. There is greater or lesser use of market mechanisms, private ownership, wage incentives and so on according to whether state planning remains highly centralised along Soviet lines or is modified through economic reforms as in Hungary. Third, the implementation of economic strategies – through whatever combination of direct methods and market mechanisms – depends on the rule of the party and its continuing monopoly of political power. The party's relationship to other forces in society, including, for example, the church or regional interests, will depend upon the specific and cultural characteristics of each country and its past record in resolving various economic and political problems.

Together, these three factors account for a varied pattern of state socialism which includes remarkable contrasts both within countries (for example, between widespread religious adherence and the official ideology of atheism in Poland) and between countries such as East Germany and Hungary, with their alternative approaches to economic planning. Some elements of this pattern are especially significant because they represent not just the legacy of a country's history and culture on the path of development but choices which may ultimately decide the future shape of state socialism as a whole. The task of this chapter is to show how the state socialist countries have responded to the imperatives of industrialisation and socialist ideology with varied effects on the dynamics of accumulation and class relations.

In its level of industrial development, East Germany ranks as the leading state socialist country, equal to many of those in Western Europe. By contrast, Bulgaria, Romania and Poland continue to have large agricultural populations. Indicators of these different levels of industrialisation are shown in table 7.

Clearly, the level of industrialisation has profound significance for political and social management. This was clearly reflected in the development priorities of state socialism in the Soviet Union. The total commitment to rapid industrialisation led to the adoption of a variety of economic strategies ranging from the use of market mechanisms and incentives of the NEP, to the coercive methods of the first Five Year Plan and the institutions of the present planning system. Variations on the same themes are evident throughout the countries of Eastern Europe. Each country has implemented policies of land reform, agricultural reorganisation and industrial development in the light of its own particular circumstances. Where there is a large agricultural population as in Poland or Romania, for example, land ownership and farming methods are less fully

TABLE 7   PERCENTAGE OF WORKING POPULATION IN
MAJOR INDUSTRIAL SECTORS IN 1978

	Bulgaria	Hungary	GDR	Poland	Romania	USSR	Czecho-slovakia
Material production sector (total)	83.5	81.9	81.0	86.6	88.0	77.4	80.0
Industry and construction	42.9	42.8	51.0	39.1	42.4	38.5	48.1
Agriculture and forestry	25.2	21.7	10.6	30.8	32.8	20.9	14.5
Transportation and com-munications	6.8	8.0	7.5	6.4	5.9	9.0	6.7
Trade, material and technical supplies, service and procurements	8.2	9.4	10.7	7.6	6.0	7.9	10.5
Non-productive sector	16.5	18.1	19.0	13.4	12.0	22.6	20.0

Source: Council for Mutual Economic Assistance, 1979.

socialised that in countries where a large proportion of the former
agricultural population has been absorbed into the industrial
sector. The Soviet strategy of rapid collectivisation by the use
of force has not been repeated in these other countries. Throughout
Eastern Europe there is a wide variation: in Poland more than
three-quarters of agricultural production is officially described as
'non-socialist', while in East Germany the farming sector is the
most highly advanced and collectivised. Hungary is at an intermediate stage of industrial development, with a distribution of

agricultural land which reflects both the land reforms implemented
after 1945 and the relatively low level of state ownership. This is
shown in table 8.

TABLE 8   OWNERSHIP OF AGRICULTURAL LAND
IN HUNGARY

	In thousands of hectares	*As % of total*
State sector	1,018	15.4
Cooperative sector	5,180	78.2
Cooperative farms	4,652	70.2
Household plots	368	5.6
Private farms	428	6.4

Source: Central Statistical Office, 1982

State farms in Hungary, which are on average double the size
of cooperative farms, are managed by appointees of the ministry
of agriculture, which specifies what is to be produced. Workers on
these farms are paid wages, plus bonuses, and are members of a
trade union. On cooperative farms, which work more than 70 per
cent of the country's agricultural land, decisions about what to
produce are made locally and wages fluctuate according to the farm's
output and its ability to sell its products. In addition to the small
residual number of privately owned farms, each cooperative farm
worker is entitled to a small private plot of land. Productivity on
these tends to be high so that there is little incentive for the state
to press for the further socialisation of agriculture.

The Hungarian case, then, illustrates that the pattern of socialist
development is not simply a gradual implementation of the Soviet
model of comprehensive state ownership and control. In fact, this
has only occurred in those countries which were already highly
industrialised when they were incorporated into the Soviet bloc after
the Second World War; that is, East Germany and Czechoslovakia.
Elsewhere, the goal of economic policy has been to industrialise
as rapidly as possible. Consequently, the socialist reorganisation
of agriculture has taken second place to the construction of an
industrial infrastructure. In Hungary, for example, there was an

attempt in the 1950s to transform a mixed agrarian and industrial structure into a predominantly industrial structure within the space of a single five-year plan. For this reason, annual investment into agriculture was limited to 13 per cent of the total (Huszár et al., 1978, pp. 134-5). This emphasis on industrial investment has continued even though the most intensive stage of industrial development has been completed. In socialist terms, therefore, agriculture has remained at a lower stage of development than the Soviet model would suggest. However, by 1960, in all the countries of Eastern Europe the greater proportion of agricultural production was organised in state collective or cooperative farms. Poland remains the chief exception to this because policies designed to implement collectivisation had to be abandoned in the face of strong resistance from the peasantry. The relative lack of state control over the agricultural sector has been a significant causal factor behind the problems which have beset the Polish economy.

While there are differences between countries in the development of agriculture, there is a shared pattern of industrial development based on the Soviet experience of central planning. The implementation of state ownership and control was more rapid than in the Soviet Union and was largely complete in all the countries of Eastern Europe by the late 1950s. However, the industrial infrastructures which existed prior to the transition of state socialism have given rise to some differences. In Poland, Czechoslovakia and East Germany these stem from the fact that industrial development prior to 1945 had occurred with a considerable amount of direct and indirect encouragement from the state. Enterprises in basic industries were relatively large, and many were state-owned or accustomed to state intervention; this facilitated their incorporation into a centrally planned state socialist economy. In Czechoslovakia and East Germany post-war growth depended as much on improved industrial productivity as on the expansion of the industrial labour force. Elsewhere in Eastern Europe, the impact of socialist industrialisation was felt initially in terms of large-scale migration of labour from the land into new urban industries.

Notwithstanding these differences, the essential features of economic planning in the industrialised and less industrialised countries of Eastern Europe were modelled directly on the Soviet Union until the late 1950s and early 1960s. It was only after two decades of state socialism in a variety of national forms that new models of planning were developed. They emerged as a response to the built-in constraints which confronted each state socialist economy as it attempted to expand its productive forces; for instance, those to do with the inflexibility of the economic plan, those arising from the centralisation and rigidity of political control, and those of low productivity in the agricultural sector. However, since the state apparatus in each country is ultimately committed to maintaining its political supremacy and retains ownership and control of the major means of production, any national differences are best regarded as points on a continuum rather than distinct alternatives to the Moscow blueprint. At the one end are those societies where a highly centralised system of economic planning and control still prevails, while at the other are those where market mechanisms are used on a wide scale to reconcile supply and demand, and where material incentives play an important role in stimulating production. Before considering the impact of the 'socialist market' system on the social structures of East European countries, it is necessary to describe how it was adopted as a major modification of the direct 'command' system.

In those centrally planned economies which most closely approximate the Stalinist model, priorities are determined by state officials who set quantitative targets for all industries. Individual production units are then obliged to meet their share of these general targets. Centralised planning decisions of this kind are shaped less by detailed economic information than by broad social and ideological goals. This is the key to understanding the reformist tendencies in the state socialist economies. In the 1950s, when state planning involved the regulation of basic industries producing a limited range of standardised goods, the setting of output targets according to a general plan was an effective mechanism for mobilising resources and ensuring that urgent priorities such as the construction of heavy industries were met. However, economic expansion not only led to increased output, more advanced technology and a large industrial labour force, but it also brought a new scale of complexity into the planning process.

Growth in the centrally planned economies has resulted in several major problems of bureaucratic organisation.[1] First, there has been a proliferation of rules and regulations to cope with special and exceptional circumstances. In practice, though, too much formal regulation is counter-productive because it tends to inhibit flexible and creative responses to new situations and problems. Second, highly centralised administration in complex organisations fosters inefficiency and leads to delays as decisions are passed upwards for approval. Third, the goals of the planning system tend to be measured by indicators of quantity rather than quality. There is, for example, a preference for physical indicators like quantities of cement or number of shoes, irrespective of the quality of the products or consumers' preferences. Fourth, bureaucracies tend to acquire defence mechanisms and to create veils of secrecy against moves for change and reform. When administrative and political power are combined as in Soviet-type societies, these defence mechanisms are exceptionally strong. Finally, with higher levels of industrial development, the proportion of mental relative to manual labour increases. The output of these workers is often less amenable to measurement, and methods of direct supervision are less easy to apply.

In short, as far as economic management is concerned – and many of the inefficiencies of bureaucratic centralisation apply equally to other aspects of life in state socialist societies including education, urban planning and the media – it has become increasingly clear that the coordination of a highly complex industrial system and division of labour cannot be achieved solely by the application of laws and regulations. At one level, this can be understood as a problem of economic management which can be resolved by improvements in central planning undertaken with the help of large computers and econometric techniques. The alternative is to reduce the need for planning by placing a greater reliance on the market mechanism for equilibrating supply and demand. In fact, all the state socialist societies of Eastern Europe, including the USSR, have taken various steps in this direction.

However, the extent and impact of these reforms cannot be understood solely as economic issues. Inevitably, such strategies are exclusively shaped by the dictatorial party-state, which has a strict monopoly on economic decision-making. The major political factor which created a favourable climate for economic reforms was the death of Stalin in 1953 and the period of 'de-Stalinisation' which followed Khrushchev's speech to the 20th Congress of the CPSU in

1956. Among other things, the speech urged the restoration of 'socialist democracy' to counter the effects of Stalin's despotism (reproduced in Lane, 1978, pp. 87-97). The relaxation of political controls which followed not only in the USSR but throughout the whole of Eastern Europe coincided with a levelling off in the high rates of economic growth which had been characteristic of the first phase of state socialist industrialisation. Therefore, stagnating growth and political relaxation were the convergent circumstances which formed the background to the introduction of market socialism in Eastern Europe. In contrast to the earlier phase of development in these countries, the timing and the nature of economic reforms were not copied from the Soviet Union. Between 1953 and 1968, there was a measure of economic reform in the Soviet Union including some decentralisation after 1957, but the general pattern was one of country-by-country reforms, each with a different character depending on national economic and political circumstances. Even in the 1980s, movements towards market socialism do not have a common theoretical basis or a uniform pattern of institutional arrangements.

The earliest reforms were mainly directed towards simplifying management structures through decentralisation. In the Soviet Union and East Germany, for example, against a background of declining rates of growth, associations or combines were established in the early 1960s, with the aim of improving management efficiency, linking research and development with production and extending the use of profit-and-loss accounting (Holmes, 1981, ch. 1). In effect, the decentralisation was from the planning ministries to sub-branches of industry, and not to individual enterprises. these industrial associations represent a shift in the focus of control and initiative designed to enhance the efficiency of those officials most closely concerned with the implementation of the Plan, but without fundamental modification of the command principle (Littlejohn, 1984, pp. 131–5).

By the 1970s, and by default rather than design, there had been a significant expansion of what is known in the Soviet Union as the 'second' or 'counter-economy' (Lane, 1978, pp. 282–3). This is an extensive parallel economic system which operates on market lines to smooth out the rigidities of the planned economy. It includes officially sanctioned private enterprises such as small private plots and licensed craft production, as well as semi-legal and illegal markets. The latter tend to arise when the official price of a commodity is set by the government at a level which does not correspond to the demand for it. Thus clothes, furniture and other items which are under-priced may quickly disappear from the shops and be sold in illegal markets at a higher price. So far, in the Soviet Union at least, the persistence of this 'second economy' has not provoked the government into reforms which would bring these exchanges into the realm of officially sanctioned market relations. Rather, the response has been, on the one hand, to attack speculation and corruption and, on the other, to develop planning measures which take greater account of customers' preferences.

The most developed examples of market socialism are Czechoslovakia and Hungary. Conditions in Czechoslovakia in the early 1960s were especially ripe for reform. There was a particularly severe decline in the rate of economic growth and national income actually fell in 1963. In the same period, the de-Stalinisation of other Eastern European countries was generating pressure for greater political and intellectual freedom in a country still dominated by a Stalinist party leadership. The chief architect of economic reform was Ota Sik, who provided a theoretical justification for market socialism (Sik, 1976). Whereas capitalist markets are mechanisms for the private appropriation of the economic surplus, Sik argued, socialist market relationships are an instrument which helps to bring production into line with demand without leading to exploitation. Because there is no private profit or class contradiction, the market can operate in the general interests of the whole society. In practice, this means that enterprises should have freedom to compete with others and to optimise their profit (in a financial sense). According to Sik, commodity prices and wages would be geared more or less directly to demand, although an element of planning would continue through the fixing of basic wage scales and prices of raw materials and necessities. Under these conditions, the function of state planning would be to set broad goals for the distribution of national income between investment and consumption and between social and personal consumption. However, at the most fundamental level, there would be no significant change in ownership and no suggestion of the state relinquishing its control over the capital market, finance and credit.

It is no coincidence that this set of proposals should have been closely linked with the political Reform Movement in Czechoslovakia. It challenged the monopoly exercised by the central planning organisation because it allowed a more pluralist political leadership and forms of participation which undermined the hegemony of the party.[2] By 1968, many of the reforms had been put into effect but they were very short-lived, ending with the Soviet invasion of 20 August. The fear that Czechoslovakia would provide an example which the other Eastern European countries would follow was too great for the leadership of the Soviet Union and the other Warsaw Pact countries. Arguably, Czechoslovakia had proceeded too fast towards market socialism to be an appropriate model for these other countries. Although the official Soviet explanation for its invasion has always been the 'threat to socialism' from counter-revolutionary elements, this was never a real prospect. The proof lies in the fact that neighbouring Hungary was gradually and unobtrusively travelling along the same road, to a point where its reforms are now held up as a model with lessons for all the other state socialist societies, including the Soviet Union.

Hungary emerged from the traumatic experience of the 1956 Soviet invasion with a modified form of Stalinism. Unlike the reforms which took place in Czechoslovakia, the New Economic Mechanism (NEM) established in Hungary in 1968 was strictly economic and unaccompanied by any reform in the political or ideological spheres. Nonetheless, it brought about significant changes by allowing market mechanisms to regulate a wide range of economic activity. The NEM has a number of features. First, it gives a large measure of autonomy to state enterprises. Within the broad objectives of the Plan, they have freedom to decide on production targets, purchasing and sales. They are not affected by planning indicators, although they are subject to indirect state influence through fiscal and financial policies. Second, the NEM allows for some decentralisation in industrial investment decisions. While investment in the infrastructure and large-scale development projects is reserved for centralised state decision-making, considerable funds for capital formation are left to the discretion of enterprises. The third element of the reforms relates to foreign trade. Formerly, this was subject to obligatory planning indicators like any other sector of the economy. The NEM abolished these and encouraged the development of trade with more flexible forms of regulation such as import duties and export subsidies. For the small Hungarian economy, the expansion of foreign trade has been a major factor in its economic growth and the country is now more fully integrated into the world market than any other in Eastern Europe. Fourth, there has been a reform of pricing policy to ensure that prices reflect the costs of production, on the one hand, and their competitiveness and quality from the customer's point of view, on the other. The close relationship between Plan and market which is characteristic of the NEM is clearly seen in the distinction between *fixed*, *limited* and *free* prices. The prices of basic materials, key products and most foodstuffs continue to be fixed by the state. In other areas, prices are limited to the extent of their upward or downward movement. The remainder are allowed to float freely.

The extent to which the market and the Plan can be harmonised in Hungary or any other East European country remains a matter for speculation. However, for the present, it is clear that the positive economic outcome of the Hungarian experiment in market socialism has not depended upon the abolition of the command system, but on the use of the market as an instrument for the realisation of the Plan in such a way that the party's leading role and right to control all areas of life has not been seriously challenged. Thus the limits to further market reform are political rather than economic. Consequently, the future of the Hungarian system and the likelihood of its implementation in other state socialist countries turns upon the continuity of the party hierarchies.

The negative effects of centralised economic planning have been felt by all social groups within East European countries. At the highest level, the party elite confronts political problems such as the tension between accumulation and personal consumption and the increasing difficulty of bureaucratic control. Clearly, if the most serious economic problems cannot be solved, it is impossible to maintain political power indefinitely. The remainder of the administrative class – experts, technical decision-makers, enterprise managers and so on – benefit most if their tasks are made less dependent on directives and rules from above. So it is not surprising that they have been some of the most enthusiastic supporters of economic reform. The relaxation of economic controls also opened the way for them to benefit from material incentives and improved access to consumer goods. In fact, in Czechoslovakia during the 1970s, and to a lesser extent elsewhere, market socialism became a focus of ideological commitment for many decision-makers and such members of the intelligentsia as writers, journalists and students.

It is a feature of economic reforms that the working class in state socialist societies has generally been the least involved and the last to benefit. There has been no increase in participation and rarely any improvement in wages apart from the benefits of the general increase in living standards. In Czechoslovakia the conflict over reforms in 1968 was not so much between the administrative class and the working class as between two sectors of the party and administrative class. In Poland, by contrast, reforms have been largely shaped by pressures from the subordinate classes. Peasant producers and workers in heavy industries have actively resisted price rises and other features of the central planning system, which has encountered a crisis of accumulation. The dynamics of this crisis, together with the role of popular movements in the political and economic transformation of Poland and other state socialist societies, will be considered in chapter 8.

Clearly, then, where market mechanisms have been used extensively for economic management in state socialist societies, they invariably operate within the framework of a central Plan. If there is any doubt about the effectiveness of market mechanisms, state officials can override them and reimpose traditional planning methods. In every case of reform, the new economic mechanisms have been an adaptive response by the authorities to the problem of state socialist management as these countries enter an advanced stage of industrial development. They are not the outcome of class conflict over such fundamental issues as the direction of capital accumulation or the distribution of the economic surplus. Differences between countries in the pattern of reforms can be attributed to national problems of economic development rather than to any desire to depart from the principles of state socialist ownership and control. But any analysis of differences between countries must consider the effects which the various strategies of economic development have had upon the respective social structures, including the distribution of income, welfare provision, social mobility and the exercise of power by the party.

Income is the most important single determinant of life chances.

The general picture of income inequalities which was presented in chapter 6 showed a broadly similar pattern across the range of state socialist societies and highlighted the fact that income differentials are less marked than in capitalist countries. However, there are some noteworthy differences between countries.[3] In all the countries, the years immediately after the socialisation of ownership under the rule of the Communist Party were typically a period of income equalisation accompanied by a more or less explicitly egalitarian ideology. Subsequently, there has been a general reversal of these trends to allow material incentives to play a greater role in motivating workers and encouraging efficiency. The need for large wage differentials was acknowledged by Stalin in the 1930s and incentives were incorporated into the centralised planning system. Theories of market socialism also involved a critique of egalitarianism and these led to the implementation of wage policies which would allow income differentials to widen. Whether this is actually occurring in the years of de-Stalinisation and economic reform can be judged from table 9, which provides data for five countries.

The most obvious trend is the decrease in the range of inequality, particularly in the Soviet Union. Of the groups included in the table, the intelligentsia continues to be the best-paid group, although its relative position has declined. There is a clear improvement in the position of workers in state agriculture, especially in Hungary where the general level of wages in the countryside is similar to that in the cities. With the exception of Poland, which has the widest range of differentials, the position of routine non-manuals is below that of workers and shows no significant improvement. Taking these figures as a whole, there is no evidence to suggest that economic reforms implemented between 1960 and 1973 have made any significant impact upon income differentials or created major differences between countries. In fact, the evidence points in the opposite direction – that is, towards the diminution of income inequalities. It would seem that the objective of the central Plan to maintain stability in the wages system, to avoid politically unacceptable differentials and to minimise inflationary pressures has prevented income inequalities from developing, even to the extent envisaged by some of the theorists of economic reform and market socialism.

There are two views about the role of social policy in redistributing

TABLE 9 AVERAGE PAY, BY OCCUPATIONAL CATEGORY: INTELLIGENTSIA, ROUTINE NON-MANUALS AND WORKERS, ALL IN STATE INDUSTRY; 'PEASANTS' (WORKERS IN STATE SOCIALIST AGRICULTURE)

	1960	*1965*	*1970*	*1973*
Bulgaria				
Intelligentsia	142.1	145.0	140.3	132.1
Routine non-manual	93.8	100.3	102.5	95.5
Worker	100.0	100.0	100.0	100.0
Peasant	92.1	84.7	86.2	91.5
Czechoslovakia				
Intelligentsia	116.8	120.2	121.6	120.4
Routine non-manual	77.0	77.1	81.8	81.3
Worker	100.0	100.0	100.0	100.0
Peasant	79.2	85.5	95.0	98.1
Hungary				
Intelligentsia	157.2	155.1	150.7	142.4
Routine non-manual	94.8	96.0	96.5	92.4
Worker	100.0	100.0	100.0	100.0
Peasant	NA	88.1	100.0	94.1
Poland				
Intelligentsia	156.7	161.0	150.0	144.3
Routine non-manual	105.1	108.0	102.8	100.1
Worker	100.0	100.0	100.0	100.0
Peasant	NA	72.0	75.0	77.5
USSR				
Intelligentsia	150.9	145.9	136.3	134.1
Routine non-manual	82.1	84.4	85.5	84.5
Worker	100.0	100.0	100.0	100.0
Peasant	57.7	71.2	75.4	76.5

NA = not available
Source: Connor, 1979, p. 231.

resources in state socialist countries. On the one hand, it is argued that transfer payments and welfare should reflect inequalities between social groups rather than be used as a means of redistribution. On the other, it is claimed that benefits in both cash and kind should be distributed according to need and that their purpose should be to counteract, at least to a certain extent, employment-related inequalities. The resources committed to social consumption, that is to cash transfers and the provision of free services, provide the basis for an assessment of these alternative views. The examples chosen are the Soviet Union and Hungary, which highlight the contrast between highly centralised and market socialist systems.

In the Soviet Union, social consumption is financed by the Social Insurance Fund and the state budget. The former depends on a more or less proportional payroll tax, and the latter on a regressive turnover tax on such items as bread. Since the 1940s when nearly two-thirds of total social consumption was financed by the state budget, there has been a shift from this highly regressive form of financing towards the more neutral method of spreading costs in closer proportion to income by means of cash transfers. However, there is little evidence, as yet, of a commitment to a progressive system in which the costs of social consumption would be met by those with higher incomes. Table 10 shows how social consumption expenditure according to Soviet definitions has evolved in that country between 1940 and 1980.

The most prominent feature of table 10 is the relative importance of pensions and other cash transfers. The main forms of public consumption, particularly education and health, have suffered a relative decline, even though there was a five-fold increase in per-capita expenditure on all forms of social consumption between 1950 and 1980. While it has to be acknowledged that the impact of any country's social policy will depend on the resources available to it, this pattern of expenditure is consistent with the principles of financing; namely, that the objective of social policy is to alleviate the particular problems of the elderly, the disabled and so on, and that it is not intended to bring about a fundamental redistribution of income. At most, it is only slightly progressive.[4]

Hungary provides a basis for assessing the impact of social policy under a different form of state socialist regime. Direct comparisons with the Soviet Union are not possible, but a major survey in 1967

TABLE 10   SOCIAL CONSUMPTION EXPENDITURE:
USSR, 1940–80
(PERCENTAGES UNLESS OTHERWISE INDICATED)

	1940	1950	1960	1970	1980
Total expenditure (thousand million roubles)	4.6	13.0	27.3	63.9	116.5
Total cash transfers	33.8	44.6	49.4	51.0	53.9
Pensions	6.5	18.5	26.0	25.2	28.3
Allowances	10.9	9.2	9.5	9.6	9.4
Stipends	4.3	3.8	2.2	2.0	2.2
Holiday pay[a]	12.1	13.1	11.7	14.2	14.0
Education	39.1	33.8	26.7	27.1	24.9
Medical care, etc.	21.7	16.9	18.3	15.5	14.8
Social security	2.2	0.8	1.1	0.8	1.4
Housing subsidies	2.2	3.8	4.4	5.5	5.9
Expenditure per head (roubles)	24	73	128	263	438

[a] Holiday pay is included as a social consumption expenditure according to Soviet convention; for 1940, holiday pay was calculated as the product of annual average employment and half the average monthly wage.
Source: McAuley, 1979, p. 262

suggested that cash transfers had a levelling effect on income distribution because more resources were transferred to lower than to higher income groups (Huszár et al., 1978). However, benefits in kind – health, education, housing subsidies and so on – were more unevenly distributed than cash benefits, with the result that differences between social groups were accentuated rather than diminished. The growth of social expenditure since 1967 has probably done little to alter this general picture.

In contrast with Western capitalist countries where the future of the welfare state is a highly charged political issue, social policy in the East European countries has not been subject to attack by various political movements and reformist economic theories. The modest debate on economic reform does not normally include the consideration of political structures or social and cultural goals within its frame of reference. Since social policy does not stem directly from economic planning, there is no reason to expect distinctive patterns of social consumption in the market socialist countries. The impact of state socialist planning on social consumption has been in terms of its considerable growth, with policies guided more by short-term responses to problems than by longer-term strategies for redistribution. Given the slowdown in economic growth rates, major changes are unlikely to occur in the foreseeable future.

Patterns of social mobility in the state socialist countries are a further indication of the extent to which their structural inequalities have been reduced. As discussed in chapter 4, the dynamics of social mobility have more to do with the rate of industrialisation and occupational change than with the nature of political policies. According to the official ideology of state socialism, high rates of mobility are desirable because they reflect the emergence of a new type of society in which a person's social origins do not dictate social position and life chances. How far, then, have socialist principles created a more egalitarian distribution of opportunity or to what extent are mobility rates a function of occupational change brought about by industrialisation?

In all the state socialist countries, *structural* or mass mobility – which refers to a movement between the occupational positions – reflects the pace and level of industrialisation, the decline in agricultural employment and expansion of the industrial manual and non-manual strata. Thus rapid industrialisation has led to rates of mobility in these countries far higher than in their pre-socialist phase. Table 11 shows the pattern of mobility for a selected number of East European and Western countries. The first column describes movement between manual and non-manual occupations but excludes those in agriculture; total mobility includes those in agriculture; and the third column refers to the size of the industrial working class.

There appears to be a broad similarity between countries at similar levels of economic development, which lends weight to the claim that industrialisation has similar effects irrespective of cultural and ideological differences. There is a pattern among the least industrialised countries – for example, Bulgaria and Hungary – of

TABLE 11   MASS MOBILITY IN SELECTED EAST EUROPEAN
AND WESTERN COUNTRIES

	Manual/ non-manual mobility (%)	Total mobility (%)	Size of manual class (%)
Bulgaria (1967)	28.5	51.2	23.0
Hungary (1973)	30.2	50.0	28.6
Poland (1972)	30.7	40.7	35.1
USSR (1967–8)	31.5	–	34.0
Italy (1963)	25.5	37.0	41.4
England and Wales (1972)	33.7	37.6	43.6
Sweden (1974)	37.0	51.5	43.4
USA (1973)	36.5	48.2	44.8

Source: Heath, 1981, p. 203

relatively high total mobility but of lower movement between the manual and non-manual occupations. This is explained by the fact that these countries have experienced a large and rapid exodus from agriculture in the initial phase of state socialist industrialisation. At the other end of the scale, the most advanced industrial countries – for example, the United States and Sweden – have relatively high levels of mobility according to both measures. The 'old' societies of Western Europe – Italy and England and Wales – in the table tend to be somewhat more closed; certainly in comparison with Sweden. In Eastern Europe, it remains an open question as to how far patterns of mobility will change as these countries become characterised by a larger industrial working class. At present, the major variations in mobility rates reflect different stages in the trajectory of industrial development rather than contrasts in political and ideological forces.

How far has the opening up of opportunities through structural change been accompanied by increases in the rate of exchange mobility, which refers to changes in the social background of those filling particular occupations? This can be assessed by examining the inflows into the intelligentsia and the party elite. Table 12 shows trends in recruitment to non-manual jobs in Poland between 1950

and 1972. By the early 1970s, there was less self-recruitment in
each of the categories than in decades previously.

TABLE 12   RECRUITMENT TO NON-MANUAL JOBS IN POLAND
(% OF CHILDREN STARTING THEIR FIRST JOBS IN THE SAME
OCCUPATIONAL GROUP AS THEIR FATHERS)

	1950–4	*1965–9*	*1970–2*
Administrative and managerial	33.9	22.8	21.7
Specialists in technical fields	22.7	17.9	19.0
Specialists in non-technical fields	39.3	35.0	35.3

Source: Zagorski, 1974, p. 15

Figures for Hungary indicate that the chances of those of worker
or peasant origin becoming managerial and professional workers
have been greatly enhanced under state socialism. However, there
is some evidence to suggest that by 1973 there had been a slight
decrease in mobility within the younger generation of managers
and professionals and a detectable increase in the tendency to self-
recruitment in these groups. Among the factors which could account
for this is the operation of the educational system which, in state
socialist countries, can be used to different effect by groups with
varying cultural resources. The mechanics of this process are similar
to those which operate in the capitalist countries; that is, differen-
tial access to facilities, parental influence and children's aspirations.
Increasingly, it seems that children from the upper strata will inherit
social positions similar to their parents', if not always their specific
occupations. However, despite any recent tendency to closure, the
state socialist countries have generally experienced high rates of
inflow into various managerial and professional occupations. This,
in turn, has had important implications for the political process
of these countries.

The Communist Party functions to articulate and reconcile
political interests. Its structure is less monolithic than is often
assumed. At various stages in the development of state socialism
in each of the countries, the party apparatus has had to resolve

different problems. In their revolutionary phase, for example, communist parties have tended to be dominated by intellectuals and ideologists, but once in power the party requires skilled administrators and technocrats. At all times, however, the party needs channels of recruitment to ensure the representation of a range of social interests and to maintain its presence within the state bureaucracy and other key institutions. Table 13 shows the composition of the Soviet Communist Party alongside figures for the social structure of the Soviet Union.

TABLE 13   THE SOCIAL STRUCTURE OF THE SOVIET
UNION AND SOCIAL COMPOSITION OF THE
COMMUNIST PARTY

	Social structure of USSR (percentage of total population)		*Party composition (percentage of membership)*		
	1959	*1979*	*1956*	*1968*	*1981*
Manual and non-manual					
workers	68.3	85.1	82.9	84.2	87.2
Manual	49.5	60.0	32.0	38.8	43.4
Non-manual	18.8	25.1	50.9	45.5	43.8
Collective-farm peasants	31.4	14.9	17.1	15.8	12.8
Total	99.7[a]	100.0	100.0	100.0	100.0

[a] An additional 0.3% was self-employed in agriculture and handicraft work.
Source: Lane, 1982, p. 117

Even after a phase of rapid growth during the 1960s and with a membership of 17½ million in 1981, the party does not strictly reflect the composition of the Soviet population; the non-manual strata are over- and the collective-farm peasantry under-represented. The trends have been towards increased party membership among scientific, technical and managerial occupations and less penetration of the poorly educated groups. In 1981, for example, approximately 42 per cent of qualified engineers, 25 per cent of teachers and only 10 per cent of all manual workers were party members. The present composition of the party, therefore, would suggest the potential for conflicts of interest between officials who specialise in organisational and political careers and those with technical and professional functions. The party may, however, successfully incorporate the latter because advancement in a state socialist meritocracy demands political conformity as well as technical competence. On the other hand, there is the possibility that in the market socialist economies the power of the technocrats and other specialists will increase at the expense of party functionaries. There is strong evidence to suggest that this occurred in Czechoslovakia in 1968 where support for the Reform Movement was greatest among the technical strata and the intelligentsia, including party members.

The sharpness of this conflict has, so far, not been matched elsewhere in Eastern Europe. It could be argued that the more typical expression of this cleavage within present-day market socialist economies is a form of pluralism within the framework of the party. This is not the only source of conflict within the social institutions of Eastern Europe, but it is the most significant of those created by the economic and organisational reforms of the 1960s and 1970s. Other conflicts, possibly far more critical for the long-term future of state socialism, have their origins in the major division which exists between the administrative and working classes. Their contribution to the present crisis of state socialism will be discussed in chapter 8.

In this chapter we have highlighted the major differences in economic strategies and social structures between the state socialist countries but without exaggerating their importance. The one-party dictatorial state, which has yet to be superseded in any Eastern European country, is a powerful instrument for the transformation of social structures. All these states have closely similar goals, and they shape rather than reflect the variety of social interests because of their monopoly of power. Thus the differences between countries which stem directly from state activities are strictly limited. However, the industrialisation which each of these countries is experiencing has not had a uniform impact on the social structure of each country. The interpolation of industrialisation and national cultures and traditions has led to subtle variations within forms of state socialism.

Part III

Western Capitalism and State
Socialism in Crisis

7

Western Capitalism in Crisis

In this and the following chapter we discuss how 'crises' emerge within capitalist and state socialist countries. The word 'crisis' is used with caution since we are aware of both its ideological and its emotive connotations. For the purposes of the present discussion, it is used to describe those critical combinations of structural processes which directly challenge or severely constrain the development of particular modes of production. In every society there are, of course, problems relating to the maintenance of social order and control. The difference between such continuous tensions on the one hand and crises on the other is that whereas the former can, in principle, be *resolved* and accommodated within a particular mode of production, the latter can directly threaten its survival.

In comparing capitalist and state socialist countries, it is possible to argue that crises under capitalism are primarily *economic* while under state socialism they tend to be *political*. As we have discussed in a previous chapter, the essential dynamic of the capitalist mode of production is the private accumulation of wealth. Consequently, any activity which challenges this process is a visible threat to the capitalist dynamic. If such threats lead to a sustained fall in the rate of profit, it can be argued that the mode of production is in a state of crisis. This can have further repercussions, since with declining profits there is a lack of capital investment which, in turn, can prevent economic growth, hinder the creation of new occupations and bring about increases in the level of unemployment. Consequently, such crises extend to the entire social and political system. In this sense, then, the crises in capitalism may be regarded as inevitably *economic* if only because they originate within the productive process. Under state socialism, by contrast, the origins of crises are different in so far as the productive process is not geared to the quest for private profit. Essentially, we would argue that crises under state socialism have *political* origins, since in one way or another they are associated with planning and the exercise of political power.

In the Western capitalist countries, corporate managers and shareholders have found it increasingly difficult to make profits. This has reduced the capacity of the productive system to reproduce itself, because there can be no reinvestment and, therefore, no capital accumulation. Consequently, it is difficult for enterprises to modernise their technology and to expand production. Further, a fall in profitability reduces the competitive position of weaker enterprises while stronger competitors can expand their activities through mergers, amalgamations and takeovers. In fact, a fall in the rate of return on investment has been a fairly consistent trend in most of the capitalist countries in recent decades (Himmelstrand et al., 1981; Glyn and Sutcliffe, 1972). This is shown in table 14, which gives figures for manufacturing industry in selected OECD countries since the early 1960s. While there are some difficulties in comparing different countries over time, the trends are unambiguous.

According to table 14, Britain, Norway and Sweden seem to have lower profit rates in manufacturing than the other countries.

TABLE 14   GROSS PROFIT RATES IN
MANUFACTURING INDUSTRIES IN SELECTED
OECD COUNTRIES

	1960	*1973*	*1982*
Britain	16.4	9.5	5.5
France	15.6	18.2	13.8
West Germany	26.2	16.5	11.7
Italy	17.7	16.9	19.2
Norway	7.7	10.2	7.1
Sweden	11.8	9.1	5.9
United States	18.9	18.5	10.6

Source: Extracted from OECD, 1984a, table 23

Thus it is interesting to note that the countries with the relatively stronger labour movements have the lower rates of profit. Is this a direct result of the class struggle between capital and labour or is it because of other factors? Are there, for example, processes intrinsic to the capitalist mode of production which reduce the rate of profit? Or have profits fallen in Western countries because of growing international competition, particularly from the rapidly industrialising countries of Latin America and south-east Asia? Each of these questions has been the subject of much debate.

The explanation that the rate of profit has an inherent tendency to fall as the capitalist mode of production develops is held by many radical economists (Marx, 1974; Mandel, 1970; Rius, 1976). According to this view, the essential economic logic of capitalist production is to increase workers' productivity through the application of technology to the work process. This continuous investment in machinery and equipment is often referred to as the tendency to increase the proportion of *constant* capital to *variable* capital, that is labour. This ratio between constant and variable capital, which is described as the *organic composition of capital*, has a tendency to rise with the long-term development of the capitalist mode of production. For example, if we compare the methods of motor-vehicle production before the First World War and today, it is evident that the ratio of constant to variable capital (machinery to labour) has increased considerably. So, too, with the production of most commodities for mass markets; the imperatives of competition have forced firms to increase the productivity of labour through large-scale mechanisation. At the same time, this process has deskilled many craft activities and reinforced the subordination of workers to management within capitalist enterprises. Consequently, they are subordinated to their employers not only through the wage relationship but also through hierarchies of control in a technically based division of labour.

In this view, the essential contradiction of capitalism as a mode of production is located in the tendency for the organic composition of capital to rise. This is because it necessarily brings about a fall in the rate of profit. But why is this? If the economic surplus derived from capitalist production is a function of expenditure on constant and variable capital and if the ratio of the former to the latter increases, then the rate of profit in the long term must fall. Once the limits of maximum labour productivity are approached – and to achieve this is a major objective for managers – further capital outlays for new technology and equipment will, in competitive circumstances, bring about a fall in the rate of profit. The only alternative strategy is, therefore, for firms to enlarge their scale of production, albeit at a lower margin of profit. In fact, this has often occurred; one of the avenues to business growth has been to compensate for a fall in the rate of profit through high volume production and sales. (Hence the so-called economies of large-scale production which enable corporations to achieve profits derived from low margins on high volumes of unit sales.) Alternatively, through merger and amalgamation the capitalist corporation can achieve a position of near-monopoly which allows it to increase its prices and thereby counteract falling profits.[1] However, this can only be a short-term strategy since, if profits are above average, new competitors will be attracted into the market. In the longer term, then, and under the conditions of present-day monopoly capitalism when competition is between a relatively small number of large-scale corporations, the rate of profit will fall. The operation of market forces, competition and the production of commodities for profit create the need for ever-increasing amounts of capital to improve the technical means of production which, in turn, reduces the rate of profit. Consequently, the capitalist mode of production is prone to crisis, for without profits it lacks the capacity to reproduce itself (Marx, 1974).

Clearly, the above analysis identifies an economic contradiction as being the root cause of the present crisis. However, there are others who claim that the fall in profits which has weakened the dynamic of the accumulation process is largely a result of a partially successful struggle by wage labour against capital (Himmelstrand et al., 1981; Korpi, 1983). If this argument has any validity, therefore, it should follow that the level of profitability is related to the strength of organised labour. If trade union membership may be regarded as an index of such strength, table 15 suggests that those countries with lower levels of profitability – Britain and Sweden – have a higher percentage of their labour forces as trade union members.

Table 15 provides information on the number of union members as a percentage of the non-agricultural labour force in each of the

TABLE 15   TRADE UNION DENSITIES DURING THE POST-WAR
ERA IN SELECTED OECD COUNTRIES

	1946–60	*1961–76*
Sweden	65	76
Norway	47	44
Britain	43	44
West Germany	36	34
United States	27	26
France	28	19

Source: Extracted from Korpi, 1983, table 3.2

countries. Sweden is exceptional in having roughly three-quarters of its workforce in trade unions; no other industrial capitalist country has such a high proportion. However, this in itself cannot explain organised labour's strong bargaining position in Sweden. There are two further factors which need to be taken into account.[2] First, there are close ideological and organisational links between the labour unions and the Social Democratic Party. This has produced a coherent and well-organised labour movement which has been successful in establishing a strong tradition of Social Democratic governments. Their policies have led to the implementation of workplace reforms in the areas of health and safety, security of employment, social insurance and the quality of working life. These have improved the material conditions of employees but, at the same time, they have increased the costs of production. Since Swedish corporations have not always been able to absorb these through increasing their prices, there has been a fall in profitability.

Second, the reforms achieved by organised labour in Sweden have been reinforced by a structure of trade unionism which more effectively expresses the interests of the industrial working class than in many other countries (Stephens, 1979). The confederation of labour unions (LO) possesses an overriding constitutional authority over its affiliated unions in a way which the Trades Union Congress in Britain, for example, does not. It is a centralised negotiating body whose agreements are binding on member unions. Further, LO represents exclusively the interests of industrial manual workers; white-collar, professional and managerial employees are affiliated to their own confederations. Therefore, unlike many other countries, where trade union membership cuts across industrial, trade and occupational cleavages, there is a direct relationship between major groups within the occupational structure and the composition of the separate union confederations. (Unlike many other countries in Western Europe, in Sweden religious factors are unimportant sources of differentiation within working-class organisations.) This means that LO, as the national negotiating body, can advance the interests of industrial manual workers both at the workplace and within the wider society.

The development of a well-organised trade union movement in Sweden which is closely affiliated to the Social Democratic Party has apparently enabled workers to gain material benefits at the expense of profits (Himmelstrand et al., 1981). With increasing exposure to international competition during the 1970s, the Swedish economy is facing a crisis of profitability. Lower profits have reduced the availability of private finance for investment and this has prompted a search for alternative sources. This accounts for the growing intervention of the state and the proposals for wage-earner funds. For example, state subsidies to privately owned companies in Sweden were eight times larger in 1978–9 than in 1961–2 (Himmelstrand et al., 1981). We have already considered the potential of the wage-earner funds for changing Swedish capitalism; the increasing intervention of the state raises similar issues, which will be considered later.

Does Britain, like Sweden, have a low rate of profit because of an influential labour movement? If the structure and organisation of Swedish unionism provide the basis for political influence in the wider society, British trade unionism has somewhat different strengths. Although it is ideologically and organisationally less effective as a political force, it exercises considerable influence in the workplace (Crouch, 1982). This, coupled with a strong tradition of workshop organisation, has given workers the ability to obtain concessions from employers. Although the highly fragmented and decentralised nature of trade unionism weakens its influence within the political sphere, these same factors are important sources of strength on the shopfloor. Groups of workers in the context of increasingly integrated systems of production have the ability to disrupt output and to negotiate plant-level or shopfloor wage increases. Therefore, in some industries and trades, tightly knit work-groups have resisted the implementation of stricter forms of managerial supervision, new technologies, reduction in manning levels and attempts to increase productivity. (Such strategies of resistance have tended to be more effective in the traditional, craft-based sectors of the economy, where their skills enable employees to bargain more effectively with management.) Thus industrial relations characterised by low trust between managers and workers, the conflicts surrounding technological innovation, and the reorganisation of work may have significantly reduced the competitive position of British companies in world markets (Fox, 1974). Consequently, in some sectors of production, firms have 'bought off' worker resistance with high wages and, when these increased costs have not been matched by greater productivity or price increases, profitability has suffered. For quite different reasons, then, the bargaining strength of employees in both Britain and Sweden has contributed to a decline in profitability. There is support for this claim in the fact that British companies with overseas operating units have been able to obtain a higher rate of return from these enterprises than from their home-based plants (Glyn and Sutcliffe, 1972).

These arguments attribute the crisis of Western capitalism to inherent tendencies in the mode of production on the one hand, and to the influence of organised labour on the other. But the rapid industrialisation of a number of countries in south-east Asia, Africa and Latin America has further aggravated the nature of this crisis (Jordan, 1982). Manufacturers in these countries have been able to under-cut the prices of commodities produced in the mature capitalist countries. The competition stems from two types of company – those which are independent, locally owned and indigenous to the developing countries and those that are financed and controlled by multinational corporations. The former, through their success in regional and national markets, have expanded into world markets. In some product areas, this has led to the bankruptcy of Western-based companies because of their higher production costs associated with the better wages and working conditions achieved by organised labour. But the significance of the latter – the multinational corporations – can be judged by the fact that 'in 1974, foreign controlled companies owned 41 per cent of all assets in manufacturing industry in Turkey, and 29 per cent in Brazil. Multinational corporations had a 70 per cent share of the manufactured exports of Singapore in 1972 and 43 per cent of those of Brazil' (Jordan, 1982, p. 126). Such corporations establish manufacturing units in less developed countries according to comparative analyses of costs of production. Consequently, governments are often forced to compete with each other in providing favourable 'sites' for production and this can entail the promise of strict control over trade unions, the offer of grants and tax rebates for factory construction, and the supply of an acquiescent labour force.[3] Consequently, the economic and social development of these countries becomes linked to the needs of the multinational corporations.

Such developments have had at least three major effects for the Western capitalist countries. First, they are having to compete against each other by offering inducements to multinational corporations to locate production in their own countries. Thus like many developing states they offer tax concessions, factory grants and so on. This, for example, is the practice in the automobile industry and it was only after the offer of substantial financial incentives by the British government that the Nissan Corporation decided to build an assembly plant in the North-east of England in 1984. Second, the industrialisation of third-world countries has provided channels for highly profitable investment which otherwise would probably have been directed to ventures within the Western countries. Third, the industrialisation of developing countries is contributing to the decline of industrial manufacturing in the mature capitalist economies.

A number of explanations has been advanced for this process of 'deindustrialisation'. There are those who argue that the application of Keynsian economic theory in Western Europe has brought about an expansion of the public sector which in the economic growth period of the 1960s attracted labour through the offer of higher wages and better working conditions. As a result, privately owned industrial manufacturing corporations had to increase their wage-rates in order to recruit staff, and this in turn made them less able to compete in international markets (Eltis and Bacon, 1978). There is the further claim that the development of new technologies, increasingly capital-intensive production, and hence the increasing organic composition of capital have reduced the need for human labour in industrial manufacturing. Finally, it is argued that the diversion of investment towards the less developed countries has been the major factor behind the large-scale deindustrialisation of the older capitalist economies. Table 16 provides data on trends in manufacturing output in the various world regions. The figures in brackets refer to the proportion of world manufacturing output produced in each of the regions.

TABLE 16   INDICES OF MANUFACTURING OUTPUT
BY REGION (1975 = 100)

	1965	*1970*	*1975*	*1978*
North America (36%)	83	93	100	123
EEC (34%)	69	91	100	111
Africa (excluding S. Africa) (1.1%)	53	76	100	124
East and south-east Asia (excluding Japan) (3%)	51	71	100	133
Caribbean and Latin America (7.5%)	48	69	100	115

Source: Extracted from Jordan, 1982, table 4.2

Table 16 shows that the greatest amount of industrial production occurs in the mature capitalist economies, particularly the USA, the EEC and Japan. Nevertheless, industrial production has recently grown more rapidly in the developing countries and since 1970 manufacturing output in the more developed regions has tended to stagnate. This has had important implications for employment levels within these countries, where the labour force employed in manufacturing industry has generally declined. Table 17, again taken from Jordan, documents this.

Table 17 shows that, with the exception of Britain, industrial employment in the various countries was either stable or expanding until the mid-1970s. Since then, however, there has been a decline in all of the countries, even in Japan. But the most dramatic fall has been in Britain, where the proportion of the labour force engaged in industrial occupations has dropped by more than 10 per cent since 1962. Perhaps there are a number of reasons which

TABLE 17   PERCENTAGE OF TOTAL LABOUR FORCE
EMPLOYED IN INDUSTRY IN SELECTED COUNTRIES

	1962	1973	1978	1980
United Kingdom	48.2	42.6	39.5	37.7
West Germany	49.7	49.5	45.0	44.9
United States	31.7	33.2	31.2	30.2
Japan	31.2	37.2	35.0	35.6
France	38.5	39.3	36.9	36.4

Source: Extracted from Jordan, 1982, table 3.3

would account for the peculiarities of the British case. We have
already noted the strength of 'shopfloor' unionism but other pertinent
factors could be the loss of colonial territories and their preferential
markets, the lack of an entrepreneurial culture and the antipathy
of City institutions towards manufacturing investment.

Arguments which seek to explain the economic crisis of the
Western world in terms of the increasing organic composition of
capital, the growing strength of organised labour and the industrialisation of developing countries should not be regarded as separate
and distinct theories. In fact, they are closely related. The development
of organised labour has been encouraged by the growth of large-scale
corporations which have, in turn, invested in manufacturing in a
number of developing countries. Furthermore, the vigorous growth
of Western capitalism during the immediate post-war decades,
together with the rapid industrialisation of several countries, has
led to the over-production of many world market commodities. This
has often brought about price-cutting and product-dumping which
has contributed to the economic slump of the 1970s and 1980s. This
has been the case, for example, with the production of steel,
automobiles, shipping and many other manufactured engineering
goods. In recent years, furthermore, the recession has been amplified
by the monetarist economic policies of several major governments,
which have reduced their spending on health, welfare and social
utilities. Given, then, this analysis of the causes of the present-day
crisis, what are the major effects for the overall structure of Western
capitalist societies?

Because of the fall in profits, it has become increasingly difficult for industrial corporations to finance their investment programmes either internally or through loans and other forms of credit. To this extent, technological modernisation has been inhibited and the competitive position of many corporations has been further weakened. It is because of this that the state in Western countries has become increasingly involved in the productive process (Strinati, 1982). In recent years Western states have adopted four major strategies to encourage capital accumulation. First, they have attempted to reduce the production costs of many corporations by offering a variety of loans and subsidies. In Britain, for example, the Industrial Reorganisation Corporation in the 1960s, and later the National Enterprise Board, offered a range of financial inducements to encourage mergers, amalgamations and the application of new technologies.

Second, the state has been able to maintain profits in the capitalist sector by being a major customer and purchaser. In its purchasing of military hardware or heavy capital equipment for public utilities, for example, the state can negotiate contracts with corporations so that they obtain a 'normal' profit (Westergaard and Resler, 1975). Third, on occasion, the state has taken into public ownership corporations and industrial sectors faced with bankruptcy. The growth of the state-owned industries in Britain, Italy, France and the Scandinavian countries can almost entirely be explained in this way (Himmelstrand et al., 1981). The state has assumed ownership of industries – creating state capitalist enterprises – for a variety of reasons; sometimes because of their public utility (for example, the railways); for their national strategic significance; to preserve employment; or for various technological reasons. However, despite these diverse reasons, state-owned companies in Western Europe are generally managed according to criteria of efficiency and profitability similar to those which prevail in privately owned corporations. The only difference between them may be concessions to ignore the need for profit-maximisation, like their requirement to preserve railway, bus, telephone and electricity services in remote geographical areas or to maintain job opportunities in areas of high unemployment.

Fourth, Western states have intervened to support profits by attempting to regulate the wage demands of wage labour (Strinati,

1982). With the growing influence of trade unions in the post-war era until the late 1970s, the state has pursued income policies and encouraged wage guidelines (Crouch, 1979). The form and nature of these may have varied from country to country and between successive governments within the same country, but the objective has been the same: to reduce the demands of labour and to bolster profits. Such strategies, however, are chiefly necessary in periods of full employment when the bargaining strength of organised labour is at its maximum. During the 1950s and 1960s, it became evident that wage demands were eroding profits to such an extent that the state endeavoured to limit the average rise in wages by fiscal measures and voluntary restraint. When these failed, as in Britain during the late 1960s, it became necessary to introduce statutory controls. But with high levels of unemployment in the 1970s and 1980s, governments have found an ally in the market which has generally reduced the negotiating strength of labour.

For these reasons, the state in many, if not all, capitalist countries is no longer concerned simply to guarantee the minimum general conditions for the accumulation process. Largely because of the crisis of profitability, it has become more directly involved in this process. Even in Britain, where the counter-ideology of monetarism and Thatcherism is attempting to reverse the trend, the level of state involvement in the economic process remains high, just as in most other capitalist countries. Has this, in any way, affected the nature of the state?

It has been argued that growing state intervention in many Western countries is leading to corporatism in the sense of an economic system which combines private ownership with public control (Winkler, 1977). Consequently, the state's earlier *facilitative* and *supportive* functions have been superseded by a more *directive* role.[4] The *facilitative* state is of the kind admired by neo-classical economists and is primarily concerned with providing the minimum conditions necessary for the efficient operation of the capitalist mode of production – for example, a legal framework, a stable currency and a labour market. The supportive state, by contrast, provides a range of subsidies to privately owned industry. It manages aggregate demand and undertakes a range of services – education, training, welfare and health, technological research and development – all of which are useful to the capitalist corporation. Corporatism emerges, however, when the state directly intervenes in the privately owned productive process and as a result exercises control over the internal decision-making of corporations by prescribing or limiting the range of choice open to capitalist owners and managers. The directive state, then, curtails the autonomy earlier enjoyed by the capitalist corporation in such areas as wage negotiations and dividend distributions (incomes policies), the development of manufacturing capacity (town and country planning and regional economic policies) and the employment of labour (industrial relations and employment legislation). The directive state is probably most fully developed in Sweden, France and West Germany, although there were shifts in this direction in Britain under the Labour regimes of the 1960s and 1970s.[5] It is these trends which the Thatcher government of the 1980s is trying to reverse.

The development of the directive state and of corporatism in general as responses to the problems of capitalism can, in fact, exaggerate the crisis tendencies. In Sweden, for instance, the development of the state regulation of employment relationships, conditions of work, health and safety, and the general conditions under which production is carried out has led many large Swedish corporations to invest overseas in response to state-imposed costs. Thus, betwen 1960 and 1970, those employed by Swedish industrial firms abroad increased by 71 per cent, while at the same time there was a stagnation of industrial employment within Sweden itself (Himmelstrand et al., 1981, table 6.1). Corporatism has, therefore, amplified the crisis tendencies of the Swedish economy, because companies have sponsored the growth of subsidiaries in developing countries.

Because of these contradictions, corporatism may be regarded as an unstable phase in the development of the capitalist mode of production. Depending on the nature of the political regime and the intensity of conflict between capital and organised labour, it may develop in one of two directions. It may evolve into a form of state capitalism with public control over private ownership being superseded by a rapid expansion of public ownership. The proposed wage-earner funds in Sweden may be interpreted as an example of this. Alternatively, the election of conservative governments pledged to the restoration of competitive capitalism may lead to a dismantling of corporatist structures. However, the experience of the Thatcher government in Britain would suggest that the alternative to corporatism is not only high unemployment but also the decline of large sectors of manufacturing industry. This is because they 'need' state support if they are to compete effectively against industries based in low-wage economies.

The crisis of profitability in the Western countries has affected not only capital and the nature of the state but also labour. The most evident expression of this has been the dramatic increase in the general level of unemployment. The pattern is shown in tables 18 and 19. The former refers to the overall rate of increase in the OECD countries and the latter to a selected number of countries.

TABLE 18   STANDARDISED UNEMPLOYMENT RATES
IN FIFTEEN OECD COUNTRIES, 1968–83

	Unemployment rate
1968	2.8
1970	3.1
1972	3.7
1974	3.5
1976	5.3
1978	5.2
1980	5.8
1982	8.2
1983	8.7

Source: OECD, 1984b, p. 76

From table 18 it can be seen that in the late 1960s the level of unemployment was relatively low: approximately 2.8 per cent of the total labour force. During the following decade, the average rate increased to more than 5 per cent, but by the early 1980s more than 8 per cent of the total labour force in the OECD countries was unemployed. Since the 1960s, therefore, the average rate of unemployment has more than trebled. Within this overall trend, some countries have fared better than others. This is shown in table 19.

In most of the OECD countries, the increase in the level of unemployment has been dramatic; but most of all in Britain, where

TABLE 19   STANDARDISED UNEMPLOYMENT RATES IN
SELECTED OECD COUNTRIES
(AS A PERCENTAGE OF THE TOTAL LABOUR FORCE)

	1968	*1983*
Britain	3.2	13.1
France	2.6	8.0
Italy	5.6	9.7
Japan	1.2	2.5
Sweden	2.2	3.5
United States	3.5	9.5
West Germany	1.5	8.0

Source: OECD, 1984b, p. 76

government economic policies have enhanced the impact of unemployment brought about by the crisis of profitability and
increasing competition from developing countries. Among those
countries in table 19 only Sweden in Western Europe has main-
tained employment at the level of the 1960s. This is an indication
of how far social democratic regimes in capitalist countries can
provide positive benefits for wage labour (Korpi, 1983). Consistently
throughout the post-war era, Sweden has pursued policies of active
manpower utilisation with the objective of minimising the level of
unemployment, even in the face of a fall in profits and growing
international competition.

A major consequence of the increase in the general level of
unemployment has been a reduction in the bargaining strength of
organised labour. While the demands of labour may have eroded
profits during much of the post-war era, high unemployment is
now serving to reverse the trend. Consequently, capital may be
able to retain a larger proportion of the economic surplus for
investment in the accumulation process. This, however, is unlikely
to forestall the long-term decline of heavy manufacturing and of
other industrial sectors in many Western countries, if only because
the present high level of unemployment is unlikely to drive down
the level of wages to those which prevail in industries in a number
of developing countries. It is certain, therefore, that a high level

of unemployment will remain a feature of the Western capitalist countries for the foreseeable future (Handy, 1984). In view of this, are there any possible strategies for reducing, if only to a limited extent, the present high levels? There seem to be three possible political options; the liberal-democratic (or conservative), the social democratic and the socialist.[6]

The liberal-democratic approach stresses the need to free the capitalist accumulation process from interference by the state and by organised labour. It argues that through a market-disciplined restructuring of capital a sufficient level of economic surplus could be generated for the purposes of reinvestment and sustained accumulation. It enshrines a belief in competitive markets within which efficient corporations can make profits. These profits, converted into investment capital, will stimulate demand, create jobs and therefore reduce the level of unemployment. The social democratic strategy, on the other hand, claims that privately owned capital is no longer capable of providing sufficient resources in order to revive the accumulation process. It claims that present-day capitalism requires a directive state for the purposes of stimulating aggregate demand for its products. The social democratic solution, therefore, urges the expansion of the public sector in order to absorb surplus labour and to create demand for a variety of goods and services.

The socialist solution, by contrast, sees little prospect of restoring dynamic growth to the mature capitalist economies. Because of inherent tendencies for the rate of profit to fall as capitalism develops, it argues for the replacement of capitalism by socialism through the increasing public ownership of the productive process. In this manner, the production of commodities would be according to their social utility rather than according to their profitability. The planned production of goods and services according to their need would, according to this view, enable jobs to be reorganised on criteria other than those of capitalist efficiency. Unemployment would then be largely eliminated because of the rational allocation of human resources and the abolition of the endemic boom–slump cycles of capitalism (Gorz, 1982).

These, then, are the major political proposals for solving the present high level of unemployment. However, it is noticeable that these responses to the economic crisis appear to be having little political effect. Furthermore, popular reaction to the crisis and to high unemployment has not, so far, led to the formation of broadly based social movements (Seabrook, 1982). There would seem to be a number of reasons for this. First, the unemployed include groups with a wide diversity of work experiences, expectations and aspirations. Second, they lack resources with which to bargain; the withdrawal of labour in industrial disputes is directly opposed to the interests of capital, but labour detached from the employment relationship is powerless. Third, their interests are not vigorously pursued by trade unions, which give priority to the sectional interests of those at work. Fourth, there is a prevalent belief among the unemployed and the wider population that their plight is caused by factors beyond political control; namely, the imperatives of technological change and the forces of international competition. Finally, the ethic of work encourages the individualistic belief that worklessness is a symptom of personal failure or weakness.

It is because of such widespread opinions about unemployment that the economic crisis of capitalism in most countries has failed to produce a broadly based political response, leaving the legitimacy of the socio-economic order largely intact. Of course, this is not to underestimate the level of resentment, frustration and discontent expressed within neighbourhoods and communities (Harrison, 1983). Clearly, the destruction of jobs has reinforced the social dislocation of subordinate groups in industrial capitalist countries. Consequently, capitalist countries in the 1980s are increasingly confronted with problems of social cohesion. Thus the tensions created by the economic crisis of contemporary capitalism may, as yet, still have longer-term political effects. These will be the subject of the concluding chapter, which follows a consideration of the nature and effects of crises within state socialist countries.

8

State Socialism in Crisis

The pattern of structural change in state socialism is qualitatively different from that within capitalism. There is a distinctive process of recurrent crises: the accumulation of economic problems which generate popular social movements aimed at changing the priorities of the state Plan. These crises, which have occurred with some regularity in the countries of Eastern Europe, originate in the fundamental processes of accumulation, as they do within any mode of production. The problem, however, does not arise from declining profitability as in capitalism, but comes from the organisation of investment and the allocation of the surplus. There is a threat to the wages of ordinary workers under both systems but the crises under state socialism typically find expression in political rather than economic struggles.

The state planning bureaucracy is where the symptoms of crisis are likely to be felt at an early stage. The groups and individuals most directly involved in the economic planning process have often been the first to challenge the party's decision-making monopoly. Whereas under capitalism the boundaries of conflict tend to be most sharply drawn between the working class and the bourgeoisie, under state socialism it is the intelligentsia and professional workers – groups which make up the administrative class – who often find themselves in conflict with the state apparatus. The pattern and rate of accumulation, the production of commodities and the allocation of resources are the outcome of bargaining *within* the dominant group, the apparatus which controls the decision-making process. On the other hand, the involvement of the working class at times of crisis in state socialism has been more an expression of discontent at the failure of the state to achieve certain planned objectives than a challenge to the objectives themselves. This is well illustrated by the case of the Solidarity trade union movement in Poland in the early 1980s, which declined to take a revolutionary stance even when the party and state apparatus were in a condition of near-collapse.

Contradictory tendencies within bureaucratic central planning are the subject of the first part of this chapter. They are the major sources of economic and social crises in the state socialist countries. The manifestation of these crises at specific times in various countries are then examined in order to show how social classes, including the working class, are involved in the processes of change. Finally, there is an analysis of the strategies which have been adopted for overcoming crisis tendencies and the impact which these are having upon the social structures of the Eastern European countries.

In the early stages of their development, state socialist societies were marked by rapid rates of economic growth and the mobilisation of resources for the purposes of accumulation. This forced industrialisation – which Marx referred to as 'primitive accumulation' – was a process which involved the coercion of labour, the sacrifice of personal consumption for industrial investment, and severe political repression.[1] This was typical of the state socialist countries under Stalinism. During the cold-war climate of the 1950s, a major reason for this pattern of economic development was the military-industrial competition with the capitalist West. Just as the Soviet Union had sacrificed socialist ideals to self-preservation in the 1920s, so the Stalinist regimes of Eastern Europe subordinated their other goals to that of accumulation under the general tutelage of the Soviet economic and military empire.

The mechanism for bringing about this system of industrialisation and industrial reconstruction was the monolithic apparatus of the one-party state and bureaucracy. It was this phenomenon which made plausible the idea that Eastern European societies are 'totalitarian' systems involving the subordination of all social relations to the inflexible and arbitrary will of a bureaucratic elite. However, while it would be mistaken to underestimate the ability of the party and bureaucracy to create conformity and to fragment the potential sources of opposition, the 'totalitarian' argument underestimates the potential for change. This is because the development of the forces of production cannot proceed without a transformation of the social relations of production. This dynamic, which is common to both capitalism and state socialism, creates pressures for change which rigid political structures, reinforced by instruments of physical and ideological repression, can scarcely contain.

The price of forced accumulation was paid in several ways. First, the mobilisation of resources on a national scale meant that the living standards of the majority of workers were deliberately depressed. Workers had no control over the conditions or rewards of their own labour. They were denied access to any means, such as independent trade unions, which would allow them to bargain over their share in the national product. Under these conditions, there was nothing to prevent the state bureaucracy from keeping wages at the lowest possible level. Second, the absolute priority of increasing industrial output fostered the centralisation of economic management and an increasingly complex system of planning and administration. Third, scarce resources were reallocated from peasant agriculture and small traders to industry. Resistance to these administrative measure could find no institutional expression; only individualistic forms of resentment were possible, as evidenced by low productivity or absenteeism. Finally, there were high costs in waste and inefficiency. Thus, while official rates of economic growth may appear to measure industrial progress, they may actually measure the accumulation of obsolete or unsold goods, projects which are incomplete and unproductive, or simply unnecessary overinvestment.

The impact of planned growth in the early years of state socialism can be seen in the figures in table 20 for three Eastern European countries. Industrial production, which was concentrated in heavy

TABLE 20   CLAIMED INDUSTRIAL GROWTH IN THREE
EAST EUROPEAN COUNTRIES (1937 = 100)

	1948	1950	1953	1955
Czechoslovakia	107	143	210	243
East Germany	–	111	117	210
Poland	148	231	–	478

Source: From Zauberman, 1964, quoted in Harman, 1983, p. 55

industry, doubled in these countries in the space of a few years. However, this expansion was only possible because planned targets for working-class consumption were simply abandoned. Consequently, as table 21 illustrates, living standards in each of these three countries fell between 1949 and 1953. There was a similar pattern in most of the other countries in Eastern Europe. In Hungary, for example, there was a claimed 201 per cent increase in industrial production and an estimated 10 per cent fall in total real incomes. Not only did workers find that their incomes were eroded, but their conditions of work deteriorated as pressures grew to intensify the pace of work, achieve new production norms and reduce annual holidays.

TABLE 21   INDEX OF REAL INCOMES IN THREE
EAST EUROPEAN COUNTRIES

	Pre-war	*1950*	*1953*	*1955*
Czechoslovakia	100	96	84	108
East Germany	100	46	89	109
Poland	100	85	72	80

Source: From Zauberman, 1964, quoted in Harman, 1983, p. 55

In June 1953, only three months after the death of Stalin, such conditions provoked a spontaneous and dramatic reaction from workers in East Berlin which led to a general strike in the main industrial centres of East Germany. In 1956, workers in Poznan in Poland responded in a similar way to deteriorating living and working conditions in a mass demonstration.[2] Both of these insurrections involved mainly industrial manual workers and were crushed by force. The scale of the events in Hungary in 1956 was far greater since they were an expression of popular discontent across the entire range of social groups and classes from party members, intellectuals and students, to workers on the factory floor. A national revolutionary movement arose which demanded independence from the Soviet Union, participation in social and economic administration, and changes in the political leadership.[3] In the end, armed resistance by the Hungarian people was unable to match the strength of the

Russian military invasion. Thus the most far-reaching attempt to alter the direction of development in a state socialist country was brought to a bloody end.

The events in East Germany, Poland and Hungary, then, represented a characteristic crisis of state socialism in its most intensive, initial stage of development. Although the oppositional movements were crushed, they marked the beginning of a new phase in the economic and social evolution of these societies. The new regimes which were imposed as a result of these disturbances were conservative and Stalinist in nature. However, they could not simply rely on repression and the continuation of former policies. They were obliged to make economic concessions, such as increased wages and the suspension of over-ambitious production norms. Consequently, this neo-Stalinist phase included experiments in economic stabilisation. These were an attempt to combine the old objective of rapid industrial development with the aim of allowing a slow but continuous rise in general living standards. But before long this new approach to economic management generated its own problems, especially that of controlling an increasingly differentiated and volatile demand for consumer goods through the mechanisms of a centrally planned, command system. Hence, various strategies for reform were adopted in the state socialist countries after 1956. That they were in no sense a solution to the structural problems is evident from the renewed popular protests and movements of the 1960s and 1970s.

The problems associated with the revisionist versions of state socialist planning were manifest in the bureaucratic obstacles to production and distribution. These have continued to prevent the achievement of various planning goals. Of course, the stated aim of central planning is to rationalise the processes of economic development according to formal bureaucratic rules and regulations. Some of the negative consequences of this were considered in our earlier discussion of market socialism. A common result of bureaucratisation is a spirit of conservatism and defensiveness in relation to both the means and ends of planning. The effects on production are reflected in an emphasis upon physical Plan fulfilment. Car components, for example, may be manufactured without regard for quality, for timing in a sequence of assembly operations, or for likely demand. Workers can be subject to erratic phases of intense activity in order to meet planning targets, followed by periods of inactivity. Consequently, the incentive system of bonuses and piece-work for the motivation of workers is rendered less effective by this uneven rhythm of production.

Of course, many of these features are common to any large-scale bureaucracy and there is widespread recognition in state socialist countries of these negative aspects of the planned economy. Thus there are frequent criticisms of bureaucratic inefficiency, incompetence and corruption in letters to newspapers and in other forms of public discussion. Even so, state socialist bureaucracies are subject to fewer of the constraints which, under capitalism, tend to limit the arbitrariness of control and soften the rigidities of the system of organisation. The most important of these under capitalism are trade unions and other organisations which give a voice and some measure of power to subordinate groups. In the state socialist countries, the bureaucratic impediments to production have meant that the development of the forces of production has been accompanied by lower levels of productivity and rates of accumulation than was often the case in capitalist countries at a similar stage of development.

This, then, is the background to the crisis in the 1960s and early 1970s, when planning reforms were under way in most of the countries of Eastern Europe. The underlying cause was the intractability of the political system. The continuing dictatorship of the party over a largely passive and indifferent mass of producers was in contradiction to the reforms in the economic sphere. These were creating possibilities for some decentralisation in enterprise decision-making and offering scope for managerial initiatives and worker self-advancement. Invariably, this contradiction was behind the more overtly political movements of the 1960s compared with the protests of the previous decade.

In the Prague Spring of 1968, state repression was suddenly relaxed and there was an unprecedented ferment of cultural and political activity.[4] The background to this was the deterioration of Czechoslovakia's economic performance during the 1960s. The country had escaped the earlier crisis of accumulation which had led to revolts in East Germany, Poland and Hungary and there was a steady growth in living standards between 1953 and 1963. However, this came to a halt in 1963 and the movement for economic reform gained considerable momentum. The reform measures did not differ radically from those in other East European countries but the ensuing political problems of 'socialist pluralism' (Lane, 1976, p. 163) were particularly acute. These arose from divisions within the administrative class of the following sort. First, some economists and planners were critical of the cumbersome bureaucratic apparatus and they argued that economic reforms would be incomplete without corresponding political changes. Second, there was a growing awareness among some sectors of the party and the administration that popular discontent over such matters as housing would spill over to widespread open dissent unless policies were changed. Finally, there were differences within the party between Stalinist hard-liners who tended to monopolise the key power positions and those who, although loyal to the party, were prepared to make concessions to the wider population and allow some measure of democratisation. In March 1968, these various pressures resulted in the emergence of a new political leadership under Dubcek.

On the surface, it appeared that there was close continuity between Dubcek and his predecessors. But the relaxation of many bureaucratic restrictions on political and economic life marked the beginning of a much wider movement. The changes were the cue for a more critical stance by the media, the freeing of literary and cultural activities from censorship, open debate on political policies and the creation of political organisations independent of the authority of the party. Many of the reforms were not approved by the regime, which made it clear that political debate should be kept within the boundaries of officially sanctioned organisations. But its inability to control the direction of the Reform Movement was a reflection of a general dilemma of bureaucratic control. On the one hand, reforms were necessary for revitalising the economy and to obtain popular support; on the other, they had to be contained if the bureaucracy were to preserve its position of power. Reformers within the party, therefore, tended to oscillate between making concessions to the popular movement for liberalisation and threatening stricter controls. This inherently unstable situation was resolved by military, not political, means. The party leaders were taken as prisoners to Moscow, and Russian troops invaded the country. The response was mainly one of passive resistance and it took several months for what was described as 'normalisation' to be completed. It involved the restoration of a conservative leadership, renewed censorship and a purge of dissidents.

However, there was not a complete return to the pre-1968 situation. The options available to the new regime were either to increase repression or to allow real improvements in living standards. In the event, both were applied. In fact, securing the commitment of disaffected members of the administrative class, such as managers, academics and journalists, was not a difficult process. With their careers and above-average earnings at risk, the party had little difficulty in securing their conformity. Only a small minority of writers and intellectuals were prepared to accept the alternative of manual work and exclusion from the major influential institutions. Industrial workers had not played a central role in the early days of the Reform Movement and they were only a minority within the party. Further, they had not formed separate organisations through which to express their aspirations. The 'normalisation' strategy, therefore, depended on reasserting control through the official trade unions and reinforcing the chain of bureaucratic command with supporters of the party line. Economic recovery during this period made the task easier since the mass of the population was enjoying a real increase in living standards. Czechoslovakia in 1968, then, represents a particularly acute form of crisis which is characteristic of relatively mature state socialist economies. It is not expressed primarily through the economic demands of the working class but through claims by sections of the administrative class on the control of the bureaucratic process. To what extent have these symptoms of crisis emerged in other East European countries?

We have noted the general tendency within state socialism for bureaucratic constraints to become increasingly onerous as the forces of production are developed. We have also emphasised how the collective expression of social discontent becomes a political challenge to the state. While the pattern of change in Eastern Europe after 1968 was far from uniform, events did reflect these crisis tendencies. In Poland, for example, during the 1960s there was opposition within the party from intellectuals. They criticised the deep gulf which existed between the party apparatus and the working class and they called for liberalisation of the political system. The working class, by contrast, was without effective organisation and leadership.

The Czech Reform Movement had no direct parallel or sympathisers in Poland, except among intellectuals and students. However, it had the indirect effect of stimulating economic reform by bringing younger technical experts into leadership positions. But the difficulty of implementing reforms in Poland was probably greater than anywhere else in Eastern Europe. The economy had stagnated during the 1960s and the party was weak and divided. This accounts for the high increases in food prices during the winter of 1970 and the drastic consequences. Shipyard workers in the northern cities went on strike and put forward demands which were reminiscent of those in 1956. But on this occasion the protesters encountered armed police who fired into them. These events brought the country close to a general working-class insurrection which was only forestalled by a change of leadership, with Gierek replacing Gomulka. The new regime adopted a more pragmatic economic strategy, promising greater resources for personal consumption and a degree of cultural and political liberalisation. These policies were successful in the short term but the fundamental difficulty of achieving sustained growth was unresolved until a new strategy of development, based on borrowing from Western banks, was introduced.

Before turning to the consequences of this strategy in Poland and other countries, we can summarise the pattern of change and crisis between 1956 and 1975 as follows. For the party to maintain its authority, for efficient economic administration and for continued accumulation, it was necessary to implement economic reforms and allow living standards to rise. But these could not be achieved without the continued dictatorship of the party. In those countries where economic trends were favourable and the party was in a relatively strong position – as in East Germany and Hungary – reforms were implemented without crisis. Even where economic trends were less promising, as in the Soviet Union, the presence of a strong party and state apparatus ensured stability. But in Poland and Czechoslovakia, where the party was weak and divided for a variety of historical and cultural reasons, crisis tendencies resulted in open challenges to the state. In neither country did the working class have a form of organisation independent of the regime through which to express their demands. Therefore, the crisis in these countries was postponed but not resolved.

However, it would be a mistake to interpret the recurrent crises in Eastern European countries as merely cyclical. While there are certain common themes – such as the need for economic reform, an emphasis on democracy, nationalism and demands for greater cultural autonomy – these elements have rarely combined into a mass social movement, except in Hungary in 1956. The Polish Solidarity movement, however, is a landmark in the processes of change in Eastern European societies because it unites the economic demands of the working class with a far-reaching though still restrained challenge to the party's monopoly of power in society. This movement emerged out of the crisis provoked by the new strategy of accumulation adopted by the Gierek regime during the 1970s. In the short term, finance from Western banks provided an effective substitute for genuine economic reform. The scale of borrowing is illustrated by the fact that Poland's foreign debt rose almost ten-fold between 1971 and 1975, from $764m to $7,381m.[5] This meant that real wages could be increased simultaneously with an unprecedentedly high rate of economic growth. Lending on a large scale to Poland and other East European countries, including Hungary and Romania, suited the Western banks, because these countries, like the rapidly industrialising countries of south-east Asia or Latin America, provided a higher return than loans to the older capitalist countries, which were experiencing a decline in profitability. The extent of this lending is shown in table 22.

TABLE 22   EXTERNAL PUBLIC DEBT IN FOUR EAST
EUROPEAN COUNTRIES (BILLION $)

	1973	1974	1975	1976	1977	1978
Poland	1.9	3.9	6.9	10.2	12.8	16.3
Romania	2.0	2.6	3.0	3.3	3.8	4.5
Hungary	0.9	2.6	3.0	3.3	3.8	5.8
Czechoslovakia	0.8	1.1	1.5	2.1	2.7	3.0

Source: Harman, 1983, p. 297

Unfortunately for Poland, the recession which began to deepen in the capitalist economies in 1973 caused the contraction of the markets which the new economic strategy was designed to exploit. But in addition to these external factors there were internal problems associated with the efficient administration of such large-scale investment. Although it was designed to transform the country into a modern industrial economy, much of the investment could not be absorbed effectively in such a short time-scale under state socialist planning. Factories would be completed while others, designed to supply them with components, were hardly started. The construction and engineering industries were unable to meet the demands made upon them, so that many projects were delayed or unable to perform to their capacity. Thus the failure of this strategy became apparent by the mid-1970s. A variety of economic manoeuvres, including price rises and import controls, were adopted to meet the debt problem but none of these was successful in improving output or in maintaining the general support of the population. The result was growing discontent within the bureaucracy and among the working class. In 1976, there was once again an outburst of spontaneous protest as food prices were increased. However, on this occasion, the leadership surrendered immediately to the demands of the protesters and the price decree was cancelled. This resulted in the emergence of unofficial groups among both workers and intellectuals and brought about a resurgence of underground publications, which represented a variety of nationalist, socialist and social democratic viewpoints (for example, Reports by the Experience and Future Discussion Group, 1981).

The increasing vitality of this opposition, the deterioration of the economy and the paralysis of the party apparatus set the stage for the emergence of Solidarity, the free trade union movement.[6] By 1979, the economic situation had deteriorated to such an extent that there was a fall in national income. The party lacked any significant measure of popular support and had practically ceased to function. The strike movement of the summer of 1980 was initially about food prices and wage levels but these economic demands were rapidly extended into political demands for greater access to the media and the right to form free trade unions. The ferment of trade union activity at both the national and local levels was a phenomenon never before witnessed in a state socialist country. For the first time, there was a powerful, organised and very extensive movement of opposition to the party. Of course, the Catholic Church had always existed as a counterweight to the party. However, it could not be described as a source of opposition; it had reached a state of accommodation with the party and it did not challenge its right to rule, although it offered an alternative focus for national feeling and identity. The emergence of Solidarity was, potentially, as radically disruptive as the Hungarian revolution of 1956 or the Czechoslovak reform movement of 1968. But, in fact, Solidarity was never revolutionary in the sense of attempting to replace the rule of the Communist Party. Its political demands were an extension of its trade union activities and its strength in the political arena was never tested to the limit. There are several reasons for this. First, there was the external threat from the Soviet Union which had sent troops into Hungary and Czechoslovakia and was poised to do the same for Poland. Second, there was the power which still remained in the hands of the middle levels of the bureaucracy, the army and the police. Third, the church seeing itself as a guardian of national identity and survival, was a major moderating influence. Finally, the economic crisis itself meant that there were limits to the demands which Solidarity could realistically pursue. For all these reasons, then, Solidarity adopted an explicit policy of 'self-limitation'.

The effect of this was to create a vacuum between the trade union movement and the state. The former was self-limiting and the latter restricted in its capacity to initiate economic and political reforms. A military coup in December 1981 filled the vacuum and restored relatively stable bureaucratic rule. Senior positions in the bureaucracy as well as in the party were taken over by military personnel. The Solidarity movement was driven underground after more than a year of open and effective participation in the political and social process. Needless to say, this outcome holds out little prospect that the rupture between the state and society in Poland will be healed in the foreseeable future, since the resort to force is a blatant denial of the party's claim to speak for society as a whole. Meanwhile, the other countries of Eastern Europe are faced with the example of a national movement which operated more or less freely outside the party and state apparatus. How have they responded?

Not all of the planned economies of Eastern Europe have experienced problems on the same scale as those of Poland in the late 1970s and early 1980s. But nearly all of them have become more open to the rest of the world through trade and investment. They are, therefore, exposed to fluctuations in the world economy, including capitalism's propensity to crisis. Only the Soviet Union has held back from this involvement in the global economy, with a subsequently lower rate of economic growth in the long term. On past experience, this option of the traditionally closed state socialist economy must lead to increased risks of working-class revolt as material conditions deteriorate. Neither of these alternatives offers the prospect of a stable future. There are indications that even a relatively successful 'reformed' economy like Hungary's can have difficulty in absorbing investment efficiently and productively. By 1980, its national income had fallen marginally, making it difficult to repay foreign debts. Part of the problem is the greater exposure to international markets which inevitably leads to higher imports. The eventual solution is almost certain to include price increases and wage cuts, as in previous crises. In the Soviet Union, East Germany and Czechoslovakia – the countries which have retained a highly centralised planning apparatus and relied less heavily on foreign investment – growth rates in recent years have, in fact, been similar to those in the market socialist countries. They have apparently achieved a greater degree of economic stability through a combination of rigid bureaucratic controls and political repression. How long they can withstand the pressures of international economic and military competition on the one hand and the demand for working-class emancipation on the other is one of the most important questions which the party in these countries has to face.

There are formidable obstacles to liberalisation within the state socialist countries, even though this is essential for the success of economic reforms, not to mention the quality of life in general. The example of Czechoslovakia shows how far intellectual and cultural emancipation can proceed without compelling any fundamental change in the state apparatus. Similarly, the case of Poland illustrates how an alternative framework of nationalist and religious values can exist alongside the dominant ideology of state socialism in a situation of uneasy accommodation. The opposition of artists, writers and academics is undoubtedly very important in symbolic terms but dissidents from this stratum are removed – often literally – from the centres of economic and political power. In practice, however, the contest within the bureaucracy between professional administrators, technical experts and party officials is of greater consequence and has provided the main dynamic behind initiatives for economic reform. Whether such reforms are of the market socialist type or represent modifications of the centrally planned system, technocrats generally appear to have little interest in broader social and political emancipation.[7] As a stratum, their security and prosperity depend on loyalty – or at very least a pragmatic commitment – to the ruling party. Nevertheless, there is an ambiguity about their position, which was demonstrated by the 1968 events in Czechoslovakia. Since the party was organised as a monopoly of power and decision-making, even the reformist aspirations of the 'technical intelligentsia' were construed as a political challenge. Therefore, while it is possible for them to demand greater *rationality* in the running of the economy and society, the call for greater freedom is not permitted.

If liberalisation 'from the top' is impeded by the character of the bureaucratic system, there are even greater obstacles to emancipation 'from below'. The subordination of the working class within the productive process is reinforced by the hegemony of the party and the bureaucracy throughout the whole social system. So there are limited opportunities for collective protest, although accounts of working life in Eastern Europe indicate a high level of resentment and personal grievance (Haraszti, 1977). For these reasons, it is inappropriate to regard the working-class movements in state socialist countries as directly equivalent to labour movements within capitalism. Economic demands by working-class organisations cannot be expressed as one 'interest' among others in a pluralistic political system. There are no mechanisms analogous to the corporatist institutions within capitalism for striking compromises between different strata and interest groups; there is only the party-state itself. Working-class emancipation, therefore, is not a matter simply of mobilising opposition to a 'ruling class' but of creating conditions at every level in society for transforming the structures of political, economic and social control. Solidarity was both exceptional and the most far-reaching of the social movements in Eastern Europe because it involved a closer alliance between workers and members of the intelligentsia than existed at any time since 1956 in Hungary.

In this chapter, we have observed how frequent crises within state socialism have arisen and been temporarily resolved. These have been of three distinct types. The first brought to an end the phase of rapid accumulation based upon the extraction of the maximum possible surplus from the peasantry and working class. The second was a crisis of administration created by the inefficiencies of the central planning system in a more mature industrial phase. The third and most recent form of crisis comes from the exposure of the state socialist countries to the competitive pressures of the global economy, within which the capitalist countries are overwhelmingly dominant. There is, of course, a close connection between each of these since they are all related to the fundamental problems of the developing mode of production; in particular, the growing contradiction between the forces and relations of production.

There is every indication that these problems will continue, and crisis tendencies will become more acute, until the state socialist societies implement reforms for making the party apparatus more responsive to the needs of the population. The evidence so far suggests that such reforms initiated from 'the top' are strictly limited because of bureaucratic inertia and the party's reluctance to give up its monopoly of political power. The alternative, which has all the uncertainties and risks of earlier mass movements under state socialism, is for workers, together with other social groups, to build organisations – including trade unions – which can reconcile the goals of increased accumulation, the fulfilment of personal needs, and greater democracy. It will amount to nothing less than a 'cultural revolution' (Bahro, 1978). Inevitably, such movements will be construed as a political challenge to the one-party dictatorial state, as occurred in Hungary in 1956, Czechoslovakia in 1968 and Poland in 1980–1. Whether the next and subsequent manifestations of crisis will repeat previous 'cycles' or reflect the transition to a new stage of socialist development will depend in part on pressures within the working class, the administrative class and the party. It will also depend on a climate of international relations between East and West in which major social changes can occur without appearing to threaten the integrity of either side's economic and political system as a whole.

Part IV

Conclusions

Part IV

(continued)

9

New Cleavages and Conflicts?

In our comparative analysis of industrial societies we have emphasised the structural properties and trends in technological innovation, economic organisation and social life which are characteristic, respectively, of Western capitalism and East European state socialism. Our approach to the two types of social system recognises both the similarities and the contrasts. It is based on the assumption that neither system is a derivative nor distorted form of the other but that they are distinct societal types with their own specific paths of development. Thus far, we have interpreted the dynamics of change in Western capitalism and East European state socialism within this broad comparative perspective.

In this chapter we continue with this approach in order to discuss three major processes which are manifested through contemporary political trends and social movements. They will each play an important part in the shaping of future social structures of these countries. First, there is the continuing development of the forces of production and its implications for the restructuring of formal employment and the future of work. Second, there is the growing internationalisation of economic, political and cultural relations. The global economic recession, the debt problems of the third world and some East European countries, and ongoing budgetary crises of the European Economic Community illustrate the extent to which economic remedies are now necessarily international rather than national. Similarly, the growth of a world-wide culture through the activities of transnational corporations using satellites and other systems of communication challenges the ideological autonomy of individual countries. Third, we direct our attention to the cold war and the extent to which the political and military establishments in both Eastern Europe and the West are apparently committed to a future of continuous confrontation as mortal enemies with stocks of nuclear weapons sufficient to destroy the human race several times over. The tools of social analysis can contribute to an understanding of militarism and the cold war to reveal causes which are often deeper than those of ideology and political dogma.

The almost limitless capacity of microprocessors to store and process information has led to much debate and speculation about the future of work in industrial societies. It is currently fashionable, for instance, to speak of a 'new industrial revolution' based on microelectronics, because the wide applicability of silicon-chip technology, its relative cheapness, speed and reliability, will eventually transform almost every aspect of work and leisure.[1] However, while many productive processes will be changed beyond all recognition, it is mistaken to assume that any such technological revolution in the conception and execution of work tasks will necessarily entail the transformation of the mode of accumulation or the overall productive process. Technological change is never an autonomous force which dictates the future; rather, it is itself the consequence of a relentless drive for the accumulation of wealth and technological supremacy by corporations and nation-states. Thus the fundamental dynamic of capitalism is obscured by the promise of a future which is held to be technologically determined. The era of microelectronic technology is new and remarkable in the range of artefacts which it provides but it is essentially a part of the continuous spiral of technological change which is fuelled by capitalist competition. It is not surprising, therefore, that current public debate about the future of microelectronics contains strong echoes of the late 1950s and early 1960s. At that time, there was an enormous enthusiasm for automation and much speculation about its likely impact on working conditions and levels of employment.[2] It is now clear that such hopes and fears were premature. In the Western capitalist countries *as a whole* there has been no overall significant reduction in the size of the labour force and only a small, though steady, decline in the average number of hours worked.[3] In the past two decades, then, the impact of technology and automation has been experienced in terms of a restructuring rather than the destruction of formal employment. In Eastern Europe and the Soviet Union there have been parallel technological trends and, until recently at least, they have experienced shortages of labour in all but the agricultural sector.

Although technological innovation does not disturb the fundamental character of the social relations of production, it brings about widespread restructuring of work patterns and a severe form of social dislocation which creates acute stress for various social groups. Such effects as redundancy, unemployment and the increasing economic marginalisation of women, youth and various ethnic minorities constitute a direct challenge to the ability of capitalist countries to cushion the impact of economic change and to direct resources into new productive areas. All the developed industrial societies are going through a period of 'deindustrialisation' (in the sense that there has been a steady decline in the proportion of their labour forces engaged in industrial production). Industries such as steel-making, ship-building, coal-mining and car manufacture have shed a large proportion of their labour force as part and parcel of their restructuring plans. Other categories of manufacturing employment such as textiles and engineering have also contracted to a similar extent. The regional concentration of these industries has accentuated the human costs of adjustment, which have been expressed in very high levels of unemployment, poverty and deprivation.

This raises a question of some importance for the short- and possibly the longer-term future of the industrial countries. Under state socialism, planning mechanisms for reconciling the supply and demand for labour circumvent the problem of unemployment as it is experienced in the capitalist countries, although in its place there are other, related problems such as low wage levels, low productivity and over-manning. But, within capitalist countries, where unemployment is being experienced on average by between 10 and 15 per cent of the labour force during the 1980s, the 'unemployed' are a significant minority of the population. Their exclusion from the productive system and its financial rewards offers a potential for protest and collective action. However, the 'unemployed' are not a homogeneous category. The greater majority are only out of work for limited periods of time, they come from different sectors of the productive system and they are unevenly spread geographically. The obstacles to the emergence of collectively based protest movements are virtually insurmountable, especially when the unemployed lose their membership in trade unions. Consequently, high levels of unemployment have not, so far, led to serious crisis in the Western political system.[4] Public opinion may recognise unemployment as a major social problem but its perception in all Western countries tends to be shaped by ideologies of market liberalism which identify both its causes and solutions as 'economic', and hence beyond the realm of political decision-making and control. Government initiatives in most of the capitalist countries concentrate upon relatively short-term special employment measures like youth training, incentives to mobility and redundancy schemes. Such policies confirm that 'something is being done' but no government can be said to have an employment strategy for the medium and longer term.

Indeed, there is no consensus among economists about the likely future level of employment. Against an optimism which sees new jobs emerging out of economic growth has to be set strong evidence that the output of goods could be increased with existing productive capacity and employment levels. Furthermore, the kind of growth which is likely to occur will probably be within spheres of economic activity which are unlikely to compensate for losses in other sectors. For example, many jobs in the growing service industries are at lower levels of skill and pay than those in manufacturing, even if there were enough of the former to replace the latter. Thus, the political implications of high unemployment may change when it is generally realised that the economic recovery will not quickly generate substantial new employment in either manufacturing or service industries. The longer-term effects may be to exaggerate further income differentials between socio-economic groups and to create a large stratum in Western society which experiences poverty, low education and political marginalisation.[5]

The industries in Western Europe and North America which have been most exposed to the impact of automation and competition from rapidly industrialising countries are generally those which have been the backbone of the trade union movement. Although many trade unions have fought a rearguard action – often with a measure of success – to reduce the impact of redundancy and to maintain wage levels, they have generally suffered a loss of membership and an erosion of their material and institutional resources. Further, the basis of worker–trade union identity has been weakened and a more fragmented system of work has emerged which makes collective action less effective. In Britain between 1980 and 1984, for example, trade unions have lost two million members; that is, one-sixth of their total membership.[6] A similar decline, albeit on a smaller scale, has occurred in West Germany, France and several other countries.

To the extent that these trends are unlikely to be reversed, there has been a significant shift in the power relationship between labour and capital. Obviously, the strength of organised labour depends upon a high level of membership, the possession of material resources and thus an ability to constrain or curtail employer prerogatives. Traditionally, the objectives of trade unions have been to increase wage rates and, to a lesser degree, to improve hours and conditions of work. But under conditions of large-scale industrial restructuring, there is the continuous redefinition of skills and work tasks and this inevitably creates difficulties in collective negotiations over wage-rates (Wilkinson, 1983). Such problems are exaggerated by the very rapid pattern of change in the new microelectronic industries. In these, trade unions have found difficulty in gaining a foothold and they have often been compelled to accept no-strike agreements. Further, while wages remain a central focus of collective bargaining, current trends suggest that greater attention will be devoted to the length of working time and the content and control of work tasks. Indeed, 'new technology' agreements may represent a first step in this direction with a higher priority given to the quality of working life alongside the more traditional preoccupation with earnings. Some trade unions have successfully insisted that work performance will not be monitored by computer systems, that jobs will not be deskilled and that night shiftwork will not be introduced without their prior agreement.

While an assessment of trends in trade union effectiveness in the capitalist countries would not be complete without reference to the impact of new technology, the main challenge to the development of workers' organisations in Eastern Europe is political in its nature. Forms of resistance are strictly limited and have not, as yet, found permanent institutional expression in any of the state socialist countries. Even the future of Solidarity in Poland remains in doubt. It is not surprising, therefore, that in the state socialist countries dissatisfaction with wages, working conditions and styles of management is typically manifest in such problems as absentee-ism, low productivity, corruption and alcoholism. Although the East European states explain these as symptoms of a social disease – 'parasitism' – which will be eradicated in the course of further socialist development, they are more likely the products of struc-turally determined social conflicts which are unable to obtain legitimate expression through collective action.[7] A higher stage of technological development will not, in itself, bring an end to these since they stem from the authoritarian, and frequently arbitrary, character of the bureaucratic system of planning and factory administration.

In the capitalist countries, the long-term future of work and employment hinges on the relationship between the market for paid employment and the domestic or household economy, where much 'work' is performed but outside the nexus of wages and monetary exchange.[8] One of the most significant trends in the labour markets of all the developed capitalist countries has been the substantial increase in female participation, particularly by married women working in part-time jobs. The fact that this coincided with greater demands for female emancipation in virtually every sphere of life is of considerable significance. Whether the modern feminist move-ment developed strength as a result of the expansion of higher education in the 1960s and the cultural changes of that period or because of an increase in the demand for labour is a complex issue which lies beyond the scope of the present discussion. But, certainly, the boundaries of the sexual division of labour have been redrawn to include a much greater proportion of women in full- and part-time employment.

It is a matter of some argument how far gender differences continue to be used to justify divisions within the labour market and how far the increased rate of participation of women has encouraged sexual egalitarianism. In an earlier chapter, we noted the tendency for women to be concentrated in the 'secondary' or 'peripheral' sector of the labour market. To judge from the prevailing pattern of women's employment and from the tendency for occupa-tions to be feminised *after* the work has been deskilled, as well as from the relatively small number of occupations in which women compete directly with men, the evidence supports the view that the system of production remains overwhelmingly patriarchal; that is, it incorporates women workers in a relationship of double subordination – to both capital and to men.[9]

The radical wing of the feminist movement locates the struggle for emancipation at the boundary between the sexes and the sexual division of labour in the productive process is considered to be but one manifestation of the fundamental problem of patriarchy. Liberal feminism, on the other hand, works for sexual emancipation within the broad framework of the existing political and economic system. It measures its success in the labour market in terms of the enactment of legislation against sexual discrimination and in terms of the small but growing number of women in various managerial, professional, scientific and technical occupations. But the relative lack of success of liberal feminism on a broader front is well illustrated by the continuing persistence of traditional gender roles within marriage. Even in dual-career professional families, there appears to be resistance to women's emancipation (Edgell, 1980). In terms of future trends, the prospects for change will depend on developments within the family – including family size, structure and relations between the generations – the changing nature of work for both men and women, and the opportunities available for formal paid employment.

In the state socialist countries, the emancipation of women as measured by their access to higher education or occupations traditionally reserved for men, as well as their generally higher rate of full-time employment, has been a prominent feature of social life. This is particularly the case in the Soviet Union where until the revolution patriarchal authority exercised through the monarchy and Orthodox religion was the norm. Even the participation of women in the political process is greater than in the capitalist countries. However, such steps towards equality in the public sphere have not been generally matched in the private spheres of marriage and the family. Descriptive accounts of family life in the state socialist countries invariably emphasise the persistence of gender inequalities and the burdens of child-rearing and housekeeping which fall upon women in addition to those associated with their full-time employment (Heitlinger, 1979). So sources of gender inequality would appear to be similar in both Western capitalist and East European state socialist countries.

The emerging divisions and patterns of social conflict in both types of society cannot be fully appreciated without some reference to the internationalisation of economic, social and cultural relations. The rise of transnational corporations has introduced a greater measure of fluidity into the international division of labour. Formerly, when colonial links were stronger, the division of labour was typically one in which workers and the productive capacity of the less developed countries were geared to providing raw materials and agricultural produce for the developed countries. Labour migration often occurred when shortages existed in the countries of industrial production. While elements of this pattern continue to exist, the changes which have taken place in the international economic system have led to new kinds of dependency and to a substantial shift in the centre of gravity of industrial production. As the rate of growth in industrial output in the advanced industrialised countries has slowed down, there has been an unprecedented increase in the level of industrial employment in relatively low-wage countries such as South Korea, Taiwan, the Philippines and Brazil. In textile, vehicle and electronics manufacturing, for example, where the labour force is engaged in the performance of similar work tasks in different parts of the world, the division of labour is very much a consequence of the strategies adopted by transnational industrial corporations and banking institutions. Consequently, the ability of any single group of workers to confront their employers directly is weakened and traditional forms of collective action pursued by workers carry less weight. Indeed, many multinational corporations have a deliberate policy of excluding trade unions from their plants.

As a response to this situation, various state authorities in the industrialised countries offer inducements so that corporations will locate their premises on their territories and thereby generate employment, although the effects of such policies can only be provisional and temporary. Thus the international institutions of the capitalist system increasingly provide the predominant framework within which long-term decisions affecting the overall structure of employment in the Western world will occur. In contrast and perhaps not surprisingly in view of the obstacles, the international coordination of trade unions and workers' resistance to supranational forms of capital is at a rudimentary stage. But the beginnings of such activity have emerged, for example among workers at Ford plants in Britain and elsewhere in Europe. It is certain that the emergent divisions of labour both within and between countries will eventually give rise to new forms of association and lead to concerted action by workers which transcend national boundaries. But at the moment the institutions of economic and political integration in the capitalist countries – such as OECD, NATO and the European Economic Community – have no effective counterparts in the sphere of labour organisation.

The economic and political integration of Eastern Europe is secured by the Warsaw Pact and COMECON as well as by the overwhelming military dominance of the Soviet Union. These countries exist in a state of dependency which severely curtails the potential for indigenous social movements such as the Czechoslovak Reform Movement or Solidarity in Poland. They are subject to the power of the Soviet political and military system as well as to their own country's party and state apparatus. The prospects for transnational movements under state socialism are therefore very slim. Even allowing for the special circumstances which prevailed in Poland, the fact that Solidarity has not spawned parallel movements elsewhere in Eastern Europe is partly due to a policy of containment and the virtual closure of the country's borders at the moment when the movement was gaining its greatest support. Accordingly, there tends to be a greater uniformity of political ideology under state socialism than is usual among the capitalist countries. This also applies to the media and different cultural organisations, which share similar assumptions and are invariably subject to strictly centralised control.

In the Western capitalist countries, the consequences of the internationalisation of culture are different, although they too share a kind of uniformity. The privately owned media comprising the press, publishing, radio, television, video and records have experienced the same general trend towards concentration and integration in ownership and control as have other industrial sectors. An important dimension of this is the growing international dominance of American-based companies. It may be an overstatement to say that 'the media are American', but the entire Western world has become the market place for the output of some eighty corporations which control 75 per cent of the international communications market (Hamelink, 1983, p. 9). As a result, there is the ever-increasing synchronisation of cultures among the metropolitan nations and their satellites in the less developed world.

This process is likely to continue as new technological developments, such as direct broadcasting by satellite, strengthen the ability
of transnational media corporations to monopolise communications
systems and circumvent traditional forms of state regulation which
are geared to controlling competition within countries rather than
to preserving the integrity of national cultures exposed to external
influences. Attempts by different states to resist these influences have
taken the form of restricting cultural imports – for example, by
limiting the proportion of foreign programmes shown on television
– themselves investing in satellite technology and providing financial incentives for home production. However, the success of such
measures requires a considerable degree of national economic independence, strong cultural traditions, and the political will to resist
powerful foreign influences. Such conditions are only likely to be met
in a mere handful of the larger, more mature capitalist countries.

The transformation of 'culture' into commodities has a double
effect on social relations. The irony is that the multinational
marketing of cultural products emphasises the universal values of
individualism, materialism, profit and competition, implicitly
denying the class character of the capitalist mode of production,
and yet simultaneously contributes to the perpetuation of class
relations. For, by synchronising cultural values across nations and
classes, the culture industries have created a world market and
system of communication which is essential to the operation of
present-day monopoly capitalism and its system of class relations.
In fact, the increasing integration of the international system does
not remove the potential for antagonism and conflict between social
groups, as the example of the transnational migration of labour
shows. This has occurred on a large scale in Western Europe since
the Second World War with the movement of millions of workers
from the Mediterranean countries to Switzerland, France, Germany
and Scandinavia, and from the former colonies to Britain (Castles
and Kosack, 1973). In the 1950s and the 1960s, when the countries
of north-west Europe were experiencing full employment and even
labour shortages, there was a flow of West Indians and Asians to
Britain, North Africans to France, Turks and Yugoslavs to West
Germany and Scandinavia, and Central Americans to the United
States. Where workers had citizenship rights in the host country

by virtue of their colonial or ex-colonial status, these migrations have led to permanent settlement. In Switzerland and West Germany, however, the phrase 'guest worker' describes their status as temporary migrant workers, although their actual length of stay may extend to many years, depending on fluctuations in the demand for their labour.

The close correlation between the demand for labour and inflows of labour to the developed countries reveals the essentially economic dynamic of migration, although political circumstances such as the persecution of Asians in East Africa and various cultural ties may also affect the general pattern. The economic benefits of migration for the host countries have included relief for labour shortage in low-skilled occupations and the creation of a sub-stratum of the workforce which is often prepared to accept lower wages and poorer working conditions than the indigenous population. The social and political consequences are visible in the pattern of intra-class relations which have tended to emerge. Although the migrant and immigrant populations are indisputably part of the social structure, they are not fully absorbed into the general system of social relations even when the initial problems of language acquisition or unfamiliarity with the host culture have been overcome. Surveys consistently show that those with immigrant backgrounds are relatively disadvantaged in terms of a wide range of social indicators such as level of income, employment, quality of housing, educational attainment and health (Smith, 1977). Further, their initially subordinate position has become institutionalised through cultural as well as economic mechanisms. Their characteristics of colour and culture have developed into symbols of social subordination which often feed discriminating attitudes among employers, officials, teachers and others in positions of authority.

The experience of discrimination, in turn, reinforces the tendency for subordinate groups to develop alternative identities and life styles which reject the predominant patterns within the host culture. When the experiences of racial discrimination and social disadvantage are sharply concentrated in particular urban locations, the combined effects of poverty, unemployment, poor housing and run-down amenities have led to outright resistance to the police and authority in general. In Britain in 1981, the riots in Liverpool, Bristol and London were spontaneous outbursts against such conditions.[10] But the acute feelings of frustration and despair have few means of expression within political institutions at either the local or national level. This is the problem which minority groups face.

It is a situation which has been described as 'institutionalised racism' since it enables the class system of capitalist society to be extended in order to facilitate the subordination and exploitation of a sub-stratum or 'reserve army' of the working class as defined according to ethnicity. In so far as 'racist' ideology is accepted by other sections of the working class – and there is substantial evidence that this is the case – there is a cleavage of some political importance.[11] Even the less skilled sections of the indigenous working class have a buffer against some of the worst consequences of the labour market, and immigration has allowed many unskilled and low-paid workers to improve their relative position. But the sense of being in direct competition with immigrant workers for jobs, housing and social services helps to account for the prejudice which often exists against minority populations. The effect is to undermine the already precarious cohesion of the working class and to focus resentment and hostility on the proximate rather than ultimate causes of their condition. Any division is a potential source of weakness and it enhances the ability of the dominant class to maintain low wage levels, limit trade union effectiveness and enable its own ideology to obtain maximum appeal (Gorz, 1970).

While the phenomenon of labour migration is by no means unknown in Eastern Europe and the Soviet Union, it has generally less significance. Movements across national frontiers have always been strictly regulated and they are almost exclusively confined to relatively small movements between adjacent state socialist countries. Yugoslavia, as in so many other respects, is the chief exception, with a large proportion of its potential labour force working elsewhere in Western Europe. The main variation to the pattern within the more 'orthodox' East European countries has been the substantial external migration of people from East Germany, Poland and elsewhere after the Second World War and during the 1950s. For example, three million refugees from East Germany had entered the Federal Republic by 1961, but they were quickly assimilated as permanent residents because of the cultural homogeneity of the two countries and the labour shortages during the years of the 'economic miracle' (Castles and Kosack, 1973, p. 39). Under state socialism, then, the demand for labour has generally had to be met by means other than migration between countries, and because of this the increasing rate of female participation in the labour market has been significant. Accordingly, the state socialist countries of Eastern Europe have avoided the social and political consequences of international migration of the kind experienced in the West.

One aspect of the global relationship between capitalism and state socialism which deserves special attention is the 'cold war' which exists between the political and military authorities on both sides of what many still perceive as the 'iron curtain'. The phenomenon of militarism has deep roots in both social systems and it is closely tied up with their technological and industrial development and with their competitive political stance towards each other.[12] From the first days of the Russian revolution, the Soviet Union inherently linked the survival of socialism with its own survival as a nation-state. This was repeated during the Second World War, known in the Soviet Union as the second 'Great Patriotic War'. While these events created a close unity between the people, the party and the state, which contributed to the defeat of Nazism, they also reinforced the Soviet view that economic and military strength were the chief prerequisites for the construction of socialism. Since 1945, the emphasis on economic growth and military rearmament has varied according to the climate of international relations but there is little doubt that the drive for economic growth has involved a struggle to match the West in the production of material goods and the sophistication of military products.

In the Soviet Union, and to a lesser extent in the other East European countries, the development of state socialism has been directly shaped by the Western military threat. The attempt to match the superior economic and military strength of the Western countries has absorbed resources which could be used for other purposes such as housing, education and social welfare. There are also other costs associated with maintaining a large internal security apparatus devoted to repressing various forms of dissidence. In economic policy, the defence sector has first claim on resources, skills and labour, and, if the international situation continues to involve confrontation between the superpowers, defence expenditure will continue to grow. One of the crucial questions facing Soviet leaders is whether its military power will be seriously weakened by economic reforms or whether such changes are necessary if its military strength is to rest on a firm economic and technological footing. These are primarily issues for the Party elite since 'public opinion' does not exist as a political force to be reckoned with within state socialism. In the capitalist countries, by contrast, defence expenditure and policies are matters of debate and subject to a greater degree of public scrutiny. However, be that as it may, defence expenditure plays a crucial role in both internal and external economic relations in the Western capitalist countries.

In the United States, for example, the close association between private industry and the armed forces has given rise to the claim that economic production is dominated by a 'military-industrial complex' which is outside effective political control (Melman, 1970). While this is probably an exaggeration, it helps to explain the fact that despite the burdens of the defence budget on the public purse, it continues to grow. Privately owned industry accepts these burdens because it derives considerable profit from its involvement in the defence sector. Further, these activities are legitimated by a deeply entrenched ideology which claims that existing or even larger military forces are required for the effective defence of the 'free world' against 'communist' aggression.

Even allowing for the need which all countries have to establish their own national identities, neither of these ideologies bears close scrutiny as accurate reflections of the actions and intentions of the states involved. Each fails to grasp the essential similarities and differences between the two types of social system. Indeed, they are directly similar to the extent that, in both, the dynamics of the accumulation process involve a large component of military production which has to be justified, not on economic grounds, but by means of an ideological construction of the 'other side' as a dangerous adversary. The chief difference lies in the political arrangements of the two social systems; the uncertainties of the more plural structures of political decision-making in the capitalist countries compared with the highly centralised and bureaucratic character of state socialism. The profound sense of insecurity about 'the arms race' which is felt by populations and expressed by peace movements in both types of society has a real basis in that both capitalism and state socialism are equally capable of generating irrational responses to perceived external threats.

A comparison between Western capitalism and state socialism cannot avoid the consideration of values and of the moral issues which inspired the founding fathers of sociological analysis – Marx, Weber and Durkheim. A description of the social relations according to which people lead their lives inevitably raises questions about the *quality* of those lives. For the majority in the developed industrial countries, the broad parameters of daily living are determined by class relationships stemming from the productive process. They constitute the basis for the differentiation of occupational roles and of earnings from which so much else in life follows. The more both capitalist and state socialist societies have become industrialised, the more these class relationships are being expressed in patterns and stresses of urban life. The classical sociologists' preoccupation with themes of alienation, anomie and the impersonalisation of social relationships is echoed in many of the critical assessments of the impact of urban and industrial culture in both types of society. For instance, there is some evidence that workers in both systems find that they are being increasingly controlled by systems of bureaucratic decision-making and technology which offer fewer opportunities for meaningful work and human relationships. On a broader scale, the same seems true of participation in the political systems of both capitalism and state socialism, granted their fundamental differences.

However, feelings of injustice and alienation have to be considered alongside the mechanisms of social integration. These include not only forms of organisational control at work but the role of the family, the educational system and the media. In capitalist countries such integrative institutions have evolved with many distinctive features according to patterns of market competition and cultural pluralism. In state socialist societies, on the other hand, there is a greater degree of uniformity because of the centralised bureaucratic form of organisation in most spheres of social life. The fundamental questions which the founding fathers asked about the quality of social life in industrial society are clearly still relevant because they are related to the nature of class and the potential for change towards a more equitable and open human society. However, industrial society is no longer synonymous with capitalism. Our comparative approach suggests that the answers to these questions have to be found within the parameters of each system and not in an idealised version of what one or the other has to offer.

While class-based movements do exist in both capitalist and state socialist countries in order to challenge the position of those who are in authority by virtue of their ownership of the means of production or their monopoly of political power, they typically emerge in response to structural crises. They do not themselves create the conditions for change. Nevertheless, within limits, trade unions and other organisations of subordinate groups serve two important purposes: they are an expression of an 'alternative reality' within the overall social framework, and they have, on occasion, successfully modified the impact of some of the more alienating features of the social structure. Developments of this kind in both capitalist and state socialist countries bear certain similarities, although it remains to be seen how far independent or 'free' trade unions and other social movements can obtain legitimacy under state socialism. If and when they do, it is less likely to denote the end of bureaucratic state socialism than the beginning of a more pluralistic form of the same system. Such a future is possible in some of the East European countries, although perhaps not in the Soviet Union, in the foreseeable future.

In the capitalist countries, where the earlier thrust of the labour movement and its political ideologies has been seriously eroded, there are indications that the more fundamental questions about the future direction of society are being asked elsewhere than within the traditional working-class movement. The 'new' social movements – as they are sometimes described – have similar features in a number of Western capitalist countries. Essentially, they involve populist action through pressure groups on such issues as the environment, peace and disarmament, world development and the alternative uses of science and technology. Some, such as the Greens in West Germany, have evolved into political parties with a degree of access to the centres of political decision-making. Most, however, remain movements of protest against the waste of human and natural resources, pollution and other threats to human welfare at both local and global levels. Although they scarcely represent a blueprint for an alternative future, they are the focus of much discussion about the future developments in industrial society. The styles of these movements are as varied as they are numerous but it is significant that they generally involve close international cooperation. In a way which was rare in the more traditional and older movements, their protest is directed against features of both capitalism and state socialism. Their vision and commitment to values which transcend both these systems allows a style of questioning and perspectives on the future which could be the point of departure for genuine alternatives to the structures of social and political order as they currently exist both in the West and in Eastern Europe.

Notes

INTRODUCTION

1 The ideas of some of these writers are discussed in chapter 1. For a more detailed review, see Kumar (1978).

2 For a detailed account of the experiences of work in a Hungarian factory which bear striking resemblances to those encountered in the West, see Haraszti (1977).

3 Such a perspective is strongly argued, by, among other, Parkin (1979), Miliband (1969) and Westergaard and Resler (1975).

4 These are discussed in some detail in part II of this book.

1 THE DEVELOPMENT OF CAPITALIST SOCIETY

1 Auguste Comte is usually given credit for inventing the name *sociology* to designate what had previously been described as *social physics* (Thompson, 1976). However, of the nineteenth-century socio-political thinkers, Karl Marx, Max Weber and Emile Durkheim are normally considered to have contributed most to an understanding of the early industrialisation process.

2 This 'scientific' approach is most clearly reflected in the work of Durkheim (1958).

3 Despite numerous accounts of the development of the early factory system, that provided by Marx in *Capital*, vol. I, chs 13-15, remains one of the most straightforward; see particularly his account of work in the factory in ch. 15, section 4 (Marx, 1974).

4 He also argued that these 'organic' forms of society were prone to *anomie* which, in turn, was characterised – for example – by a particular rate and form of suicide (Durkheim, 1952).

5 As reflected in the 'functionalist' approach to the study of industrial

organisations, industrial relations systems, and 'industrial society' in general. See, for example, Kerr et al. (1960).

6 This is strongly expressed by the 'Human Relations School' in its study of employee behaviour. For a critique of this approach, See Brown (1967).

7 Such, of course, was the kind of society envisaged by Marx and Engels (1969) in *The Communist Manifesto*.

8 For a clear, interesting and straightforward account of Weber's ideas on the functions of management within the capitalist enterprise, see Salaman (1981).

9 In chapter 7, we discuss the manner in which Western capitalism is confronted with crisis because of a long-term decline in profits which are the underlying dynamic of this particular mode of production.

10 Many Marxist writers emphasise this distinction between the *formal* and the *real* subordination of labour to capital. See, for example, Braverman (1974). According to many of these arguments, the development of the capitalist mode of production has reinforced the *real* subordination of labour because of workers' increasing dependence upon capitalist-owned technology for the performance of work tasks. Compare this, for instance, with 'independent' craft workers who are able to exercise skills and perform work tasks in a relatively autonomous and 'self-employed' manner.

2 CAPITALISM, CLASS AND INEQUALITY

1 This is particularly evident in the ideas of those Marxists writing in the 1960s and early 1970s. See, for example, the work of Parkin (1971), Miliband (1969) and Westergaard and Resler (1975).

2 The work of Poulantzas (1975) is a striking example of such an approach. For a more recent instance, see Urry (1981).

3 For two simple and straightforward accounts of the essential features of the capitalist mode of production, see Mandel (1970) and Rius (1976).

4 In his discussion of the emergence of the capitalist mode of production in England, Marx considers how the enclosure movement in agriculture contributed to the formation of a stratum of 'unattached' and 'landless' labourers.

5 Thus, the growth of these tasks must be seen as inherent to the development of the capitalist mode of production. This is to be emphasised since many observers argue that the growth of technically based occupations denotes the end of the class-divided capitalist corporation. For a critical review of the work of such writers, see Salaman (1981).

6 The same principle holds, in an analogous fashion, in capitalist-owned non-manufacturing enterprises. In businesses which offer personal services of various kinds, for example, employees' talents and skills are converted into productive use or 'commodities' which are then sold in the market place by enterprise owners for profit.

7 For a discussion of this 'deskilling' thesis, see the various contributions in Wood (1982).

8 However, this is not to deny the existence of important cleavages within such a hierarchy. Managerial and professional employees, for instance, enjoy considerable socio-economic advantages compared with most other occupational categories (Reid, 1981).

3 CONTRASTS IN CAPITALISM: NATIONAL DIFFERENCES

1 The *bruks* were essentially villages of estate workers which, for example with the discovery of iron ore deposits or because of ease of accessibility to rivers and other modes of transportation, developed into small-scale industrial communities.

2 For a more detailed discussion of each of these perspectives see the introductory chapter in Scase (1980).

3 It is important to stress that there is a wide diversity of approaches within this perspective. Many of these are discussed in Urry (1981).

4 The detailed calculations from which these scores are derived are discussed in Castles (1978) chapter 2.

5 Movement between manual and non-manual occupations has been one of the more common measures of class rigidity. However, it is of limited relevance in societies in which many lower-grade white collar and industrial manual occupations have rather similar levels of social esteem and economic remuneration. See chapter 3, figure 2.

6 The nature of these are discussed in some detail in Himmelstrand et al. (1981).

4 THE DEVELOPMENT OF STATE SOCIALIST SOCIETY

1 His views on the revolutionary socialist movement in France before the First World War are described in Lukes (1973, pp. 542–6).

2 Weber lectured on the theme of 'Socialism' to an audience of army officers in Vienna in 1918. He concluded that the socialisation of the ownership of the means of production would lead to 'the dictatorship of the official, not that of the worker'. See Weber (1978, pp. 251–62).

3 See, for example, David McLellan's *Marxism after Marx* (1979), especially part 2.

4 See Lane (1976), chs 1 and 2, for a review of these different interpretations.

5 The basic source on the history of this revolutionary and post-revolutionary period in Russia is E. H. Carr's *A History of Soviet Russia* (1950-64), published in numerous volumes.

6 Lenin's *The State and Revolution* (1974), which was written in the summer of 1917 at the height of the revolutionary ferment, gives the best insight into the relationship in Bolshevik thinking between the ideal of socialism and the problems of political power. John Reed's *Ten Days that Shook the World* (1960), is a vivid contemporary account of the October revolution.

7 The emergence of this party-state system is described by Skocpol (1979), ch. 6.

8 Lane (1978, p. 71) refers to estimates of around five million peasants being exterminated or sent to Siberia. This may underestimate the scale and inhumanity of the offensive against the *kulaks* (rich peasants) who were seen as internal enemies of the Soviet regime.

9 For a useful narrative account of the political development of state socialist regimes since 1945, see Adam Westoby, *Communism since World War II* (1981).

10 'Totalitarian' theories of the Soviet Union and East European societies were more current in the 1950s and 1960s than they are today. See, for instance, Lane's discussion of several variants (1976, ch. 2).

11 The notion of 'convergence' was popular in the period following the post-Stalin 'thaw'. Convergence theories emphasised the parallels between industrial structures in East and West, and predicted that the Soviet 'totalitarianism' political system would be forced to change by the economic imperatives associated with the modern industrial order. See, for example, Inkeles and Bauer (1959), Kerr et al. (1960) and the critiques of convergence in Goldthorpe (1968) and Lane (1976).

5 STATE SOCIALISM, CLASS AND INEQUALITY

1 See Ellman (1979) for an overview of socialist planning in theory and practice.

2 For a detailed comparison of the forms of economic administration in the Soviet Union and East Germany, see Holmes (1981).

3 See especially Haraszti's (1977) personal account of factory work in Hungary.

4 Lane (1982, p. 30) rightly points to the confusion which is inherent in the phrase 'non-antagonistic contradiction' used by some Marxists. The idea of contradiction cancels out the usefulness of the distinction

between those conflicts which can in theory be resolved within the parameters of a given social system (non-antagonistic) and those which can only be resolved through the transformation of the system (antagonistic).

5 These arguments are reviewed in Lane (1982, pp. 126–39).
6 State socialist regimes are, and always have been, repressive, but the 'totalitarian' label is typically employed as a form of denunication in the ideological warfare against communism, not as an attempt to describe the political realities of state socialism.

6 CONTRASTS IN STATE SOCIALISM: NATIONAL DIFFERENCES

1 See, for example, Andrle (1976) and Littlejohn (1984, ch. 3).
2 For further discussion of the Czechoslovakian Reform Movement, see chapter 8.
3 Connor (1979) provides a useful overview and details of income inequalities under state socialism.
4 For further details, see McAuley (1979). There is a concise summary of the arguments on welfare and consumption in the Soviet Union in Littlejohn (1984, ch. 5).

7 WESTERN CAPITALISM IN CRISIS

1 The growth of large-scale corporations has been primarily an outcome of such mergers and 'takeovers' rather than through indigenous expansion (Hannah, 1975).
2 For a detailed discussion of the following points, see Scase (1977).
3 This 'acquiescent' labour force often consists of younger women who, because of their pattern of socialisation in many third-world countries, provide 'ideal' labour for world-market factories (Elson and Pearson, 1981).
4 These descriptive terms are taken from Winkler (1977). They are helpful if only because they so briefly sum up the major ways in which the role of the state has changed in many Western countries.
5 For a discussion of this, see the relevant chapters in Scase (1980).
6 A detailed review and analysis of the various political approaches to unemployment may be found in Jordan (1982).

8 STATE SOCIALISM IN CRISIS

1 Marx was, of course, writing about early capitalism but his description has many echoes in the period of forced industrialisation in state socialist

countries. The 'prehistoric stage of capital' saw the transformation of the social means of subsistence into capital and the creation of a large mass of dispossessed labour. In a similar manner, the initial stage of accumulation under state socialism involved the amassing of capital and the creation of a 'free' and mobile labour force (i.e. free to be directed by the state). See Marx (1974, vol. I, part VIII).

2 For background to this and more recent movements of protest in Poland, including Solidarity, see Ascherson (1981).

3 See Harman (1983, ch. 7) for a description of these events. Note that this author, who regards East European societies as 'state capitalist', places corresponding emphasis on the emancipatory potential of working-class movements.

4 See, for example, Lane (1976, pp. 163-74).

5 *Financial Times*, 10 February 1981, quoted in Harman (1983, p. 221).

6 See Ascherson (1981) and, for a sociological analysis of Solidarity, Touraine (1983). The description of the Solidarity movement as 'the self-limiting revolution' is Ascherson's.

7 According to Konrad and Szelenyi (1979) the intelligentsia as a class have become the exploiters by virtue of controlling the accumulation and distribution of wealth; they are unlikely to make a U-turn on the road to class power. We would concur with their conclusion but urge caution in the use of the term 'exploit' in this context.

9 NEW CLEAVAGES AND CONFLICTS?

1 See, for example, Toffler (1980) or Stonier (1983).

2 Examples from the extensive literature include Walker (1957) and Blauner (1964). Other authors were inclined to a more negative view: for instance, Ellul (1964).

3 See OECD, *Labour Force Statistics*, various years, and Williams (1984).

4 See Richardson and Henning (1984) for reviews of the political impact of unemployment in the major Western capitalist countries.

5 The thesis that the restructuring of employment will lead to 'polarisation' of the labour force as a whole awaits full empirical analysis and confirmation. However, it is clear from studies of local and regional labour markets that a substantial proportion of the potential labour force faces a future with little chance of regular and secure employment, while an equally substantial proportion is likely to find and pursue careers in the traditional way.

6 *Sunday Times*, 5 August 1984.

7 See Alex Pravda's (1979) discussion of patterns of dissent and opposition among industrial workers in Eastern Europe.

8 For a fascinating historical and ethnographic account of this relationship, see Pahl (1984).

9 Oakley (1972) and Barrett (1980) provide useful introductions to this analysis of women's subordination.

10 These conditions are vividly described by Paul Harrison (1983). Ken Pryce (1979) gives a detailed account of the life of the West Indian minority in Bristol.

11 See, for example, the collection of essays in Miles and Phizacklea (1979).

12 The classic sociological work on this theme is Mills (1960). See also Mann (1984).

Bibliography

This bibliography refers to the most widely accessible editions from the point of view of the student reader.

Adam, J. 1979: *Wages Control and Inflation in the Soviet Bloc Countries*. London: Macmillan.

Andrle, V. 1976: *Managerial Power in the Soviet Union*. Lexington: Lexington Books.

Ascherson, N. 1981: *The Polish August: The Self-Limiting Revolution*. Harmondsworth: Penguin Books.

Bahro, R. 1978: *The Alternative in Eastern Europe*. London: New Left Books.

Baran, P. and Sweezy, P. 1966: *Monopoly Capital*. New York: Monthly Review Press.

Barrett, M. 1980: *Women's Oppression Today: Problems in Marxist Feminist Analysis*. London: Verso.

Bechhofer, F. and Elliott, B. L. 1981: Petty Property: The Survival of a Moral Economy. In F. Bechhofer and B. Elliott (eds), *The Petite Bourgeoisie*. London: Macmillan.

Bell, D. 1973: *The Coming of Post-Industrial Society*. New York: Basic Books.

Bendix, R. 1956: *Work and Authority in Industry*. Berkeley: University of California Press.

Birnbaum, N. 1980: The State in Contemporary France. In R. Scase (ed.), *The State in Western Europe*. London: Croom Helm.

Blauner, R. 1964: *Alienation and Freedom*. Chicago: University of Chicago Press.

Boissevain, J. 1980: *Small Entrepreneurs in Changing Europe: Towards a Research Agenda*. Amsterdam: Department of Anthropology, University of Amsterdam, Euro-Med Working Paper.

Braverman, M. 1974: *Labour and Monopoly Capital*. New York: Monthly Review Press.

Brown, A. and Kaser, M. (eds), 1982: *Soviet Policy for the 1980s*. London: Macmillan.

Brown, H. Phelps. 1977: *The Inequality of Pay*. Oxford: Oxford University Press.

Brown, R. 1967: Research and Consultancy in Industrial Enterprises. In *Sociology*, 1 (1).

Brown, R. 1978: Work. In P. Abrams (ed.), *Work, Urbanism and Inequality*. London: Weidenfeld & Nicolson.

Carr, E. H. 1950-64: *The Bolshevik Revolution 1917-23* (3 vols); *Socialism in One Country 1924-26* (3 vols); *Foundations of a Planned Economy 1926-29* (3 vols). London: Macmillan.

Castles, F. 1978: *The Social Democratic Image of Society*. London: Routledge & Kegan Paul.

Castles, S. and Kosack, G. 1973: *Immigrant Workers and Class Structures in Western Europe*. London: Institute of Race Relations/Oxford University Press.

Central Statistical Office. 1982: *Statistical Yearbook*. Budapest: Statistical Publishing House.

Cliff, T. 1974: *State Capitalism in Russia*. London: Pluto.

Connor, W. D. 1979: *Socialism, Politics and Equality*. New York: Columbia University Press.

Council for Mutual Economic Assistance. 1979: *Statistical Yearbook*. Moscow: Statistika. (English language edition by IPC Industrial Press, London.)

Crouch, C. 1979: *The Politics of Industrial Relations*. London: Fontana.

Crouch, C. 1982: *Trade Unions: The Logic of Collective Action*. London: Fontana.

Dahrendorf, R. 1959: *Class and Class Conflict in Industrial Society*. London: Routledge & Kegan Paul.

Department of Employment. 1980: *New Earnings Summary*. London: HMSO.

Dickson, D. 1974: *Alternative Technology and the Politics of Technical Change*. London: Fontana.

Djilas, M. 1966: *The New Class: An Analysis of the Communist System*. London: Allen & Unwin.

Dobb, M. 1963: *Studies in the Development of Capitalism*. London: Routledge & Kegan Paul.

Donolo, C. 1980: Social Change and Transformation of the State in Italy. In R. Scase (ed.), *The State in Western Europe*. London: Croom Helm.

Durkheim, E. 1952: *Suicide*. London: Routledge & Kegan Paul.

Durkheim, E. 1958: *The Rules of Sociological Method*. Glencoe, Ill.: The Free Press.

Durkheim, E. 1964: *The Division of Labour in Society*. Glencoe, Ill.: The Free Press.

Edgell, S. 1980: *Middle-Class Couples: A Study of Segregation, Domination and Inequality in Marriage*. London: Allen & Unwin.

Ellman, M. 1979: *Socialist Planning*. Cambridge: Cambridge University Press.

Ellul, J. 1964: *The Technological Society*. New York: Alfred A. Knopf.

Elson, D. and Pearson, R. 1981: The Subordination of Women and the Internationalisation of Factory Production. In K. Young, C. Wolkowitz and R. McCullagh (eds), *Of Marriage and the Market*. London: CSE Books.

Eltis, W. and Bacon, R. 1978: *Britain's Economic Problem: Too Few Producers?* London: Macmillan.

Engels, F. 1958: *The Condition of the Working Class in England in 1844*. London: Basil Blackwell.

Erikson, R. 1976: Patterns of Social Mobility. In R. Scase (ed.), *Readings in the Swedish Class Structure*. Oxford: Pergamon Press.

Fchér, F., Heller, A. and Márkus, G. 1983: *Dictatorship Over Needs*. Oxford: Basil Blackwell.

Ferge, Z. 1979: *A Society in the Making: Hungarian Social and Societal Policy 1945-75*. Harmondsworth: Penguin Books.

Fox, A. 1974: *Beyond Contract: Work, Power and Trust Relations*. London: Faber & Faber.

Friedman, A. 1977: *Industry and Labour*. London: Macmillan.

Friedrich, C. and Brzezinski, Z. 1965: *Totalitarian Dictatorship and Autocracy*. New York: Praeger.

Galbraith, J. 1967: *The New Industrial State*. Harmondsworth: Penguin Books.

George, V. and Manning, N. 1980: *Socialism, Social Welfare and the Soviet Union*. London: Routledge & Kegan Paul.

Glyn, A. and Sutcliffe, B. 1972: *British Capitalism, Workers and the Profits Squeeze*. Harmondsworth: Penguin Books.

Goldthorpe, J. H. 1968: Social Stratification in Industrial Society. In R. Bendix and S. M. Lipset (eds), *Class, Status and Power*. London: Routledge & Kegan Paul.

Goldthorpe, J. H. 1980: *Social Mobility and Class Structure in Modern Britain*. Oxford: Clarendon Press.

Gorz, A. 1970: Immigrant Labour. *New Left Review*, 61.

Gorz, A. 1982: *Farewell to the Working Class*. London: Pluto Press.

Hamelink, C. J. 1983: *Cultural Autonomy in Global Communications*. New York: Longman.

Handy, C. 1984: *The Future of Work*. Oxford: Basil Blackwell.

Hannah, L. 1975: *The Rise of the Corporate Economy*. London: Methuen.

Hannah, L. and Kay, J. 1977: *Concentration in Modern Industry*. London: Macmillan.

Haraszti, M. 1977: *A Worker in a Worker's State*. Harmondsworth: Penguin Books.

Harman, C. 1983: *Class Struggles in Eastern Europe*. London: Pluto Press.

Harrison, P. 1983: *Inside the Inner City: Life under the Cutting Edge*. Harmondsworth: Penguin Books.

Heath, A. 1981: *Social Mobility*. London: Fontana.

Heitlinger, A. 1979: *Women and State Socialism: Sex Inequality in the Soviet Union and Czechoslovakia*. London: Macmillan.

Himmelstrand, U., Ahrne, G., Lundberg, E. F. and Lundberg, L. 1981: *Beyond Welfare Captialism*. London: Heinemann Educational Books.

Hirsch, J. 1980: Developments in the Political System of West Germany since 1945. In R. Scase (ed.), *The State in Western Europe*. London: Croom Helm.

Hirszowicz, M. 1980: *The Bureaucratic Leviathan*. Oxford: Martin Robertson.

Holloway, D. 1983: *The Soviet Union and the Arms Race*. New Haven and London: Yale University Press.

Holmes, L. 1981: *The Policy Process in Communist States*. London: Sage.

Huszár, T., Kulcsár, K. and Szalai, S. (eds) 1978: *Hungarian Society and Marxist Sociology in the Nineteen-Seventies*. Budapest: Corvina.

Inkeles, A. and Bauer, R. A. 1959: *The Soviet Citizen: Daily Life in a Totalitarian Society*. Cambridge, Mass.: Harvard University Press.

International Labour Office (ILO) 1982: *Yearbook of Labour Statistics*. Geneva: ILO.

Jessop, B. 1980: The Transformation of the State in Post-War Britain. In R. Scase (ed.), *The State in Western Europe*. London: Croom Helm.

Jones, H. 1976: *Planning and Productivity in Sweden*. London: Croom Helm.

Jordan, B. 1982: *Mass Unemployment and the Future of Britain*. Oxford: Basil Blackwell.

Kaldor, M. 1982: *The Baroque Arsenal*. London: André Deutsch.

Kerr, C., Dunlop, J. T., Harbison, F. and Myers, C. A. 1960: *Industrialism and Industrial Man*. Cambridge, Mass.: Harvard University Press.

Kolosi, T. and Wnuk-Lipiński, E. (eds) 1983: *Equality and Inequality under Socialism: Poland and Hungary Compared*. London: Sage.

Konrad, G. and Szelenyi, I. 1979: *The Intellectuals on the Road to Class Power*. Brighton: Harvester.

Korpi, W. 1983: *The Democratic Class Struggle*. London: Routledge & Kegan Paul.

Krejci, J. 1976: *Social Structure in Divided Germany*. London: Croom Helm.

Kumar, K. 1978: *Prophecy and Progress*. Harmondsworth: Penguin Books.

Landes, D. 1969: *The Unbound Prometheus*. Cambridge: Cambridge University Press.

Lane, D. 1976: *The Socialist Industrial State: Towards a Political Sociology of State Socialism*. London: Allen & Unwin.

Lane, D. 1978: *Politics and Society in the USSR*. (Second edition.) Oxford: Martin Robertson.

Lane, D. 1982: *The End of Social Inequality: Class, Status and Power under State Socialism*. London. Allen & Unwin.

Lane, D. and Kolankiewicz, G. (eds) 1973: *Social Groups in Polish Society*. London: Macmillan.

Lane, D. and O'Dell, F. 1978: *The Soviet Industrial Worker*. Oxford: Martin Robertson.

Lenin, V. I. 1974: *The State and Revolution*. Moscow: Progress Publishers.

Lipset, S. 1960: *Political Man*. London: Heinemann.

Littlejohn, G. 1984: *A Sociology of the Soviet Union*. London: Macmillan.

Littler, C. 1980: Internal Contract and the Transition to Modern Work Systems. In D. Dunkerley and G. Salaman (eds), *International Yearbook of Organisational Studies*, vol. 1. London: Routledge & Kegan Paul.

Lukes, S. 1973: *Emile Durkheim: His Life and Work*. London: Allen Lane.

McAuley, A. 1979: *Economic Welfare in the Soviet Union*. London: Allen & Unwin.

McAuley, A. 1981: *Women's Work and Wages in the Soviet Union*. London: Allen & Unwin.

McLellan, D. 1979: *Marxism after Marx: an Introduction*. London: Macmillan.

Mandel, E. 1970: *An Introduction to Marxist Economic Theory*. New York: Pathfinder Press.

Mandel, E. 1975: *Late Capitalism*. London: New Left Books.

Mann, M. 1984: Capitalism and Militarism. In M. Shaw (ed.), *War, State and Society*. London: Macmillan.

Marglin, S. 1980: The Origins and Functions of Hierarchy in Capitalist Production. In T. Nichols (ed.), *Capital and Labour*. London: Fontana.

Marx, K. 1964: *Pre-Capitalist Economic Formations*. London: Lawrence & Wishart.

Marx, K. 1974: *Capital* (3 vols). London: Lawrence & Wishart.

Marx, K. 1975: 'Preface' to a Contribution to the Critique of Political Economy. In *Karl Marx: Early Writings*. Harmondsworth: Penguin Books.

Marx, K. and Engels, F. 1969: *The Communist Manifesto*. Harmondsworth: Penguin Books.

Marx, K. and Engels, F. 1970: *The German Ideology*. London: Lawrence & Wishart.

Matthews, M. 1972: *Class and Society in Soviet Russia*. London: Allen Lane.

Matthews, M. 1978: *Privilege in the Soviet Union*. London: Allen & Unwin.

Melman, S. 1970: *Pentagon Capitalism*. New York: McGraw-Hill.

Miles, R. and Phizacklea, A. (eds) 1979: *Racism and Political Action in Britain*. London: Routledge & Kegan Paul.

Miliband, R. 1969: *The State in Capitalist Society*. London: Weidenfeld & Nicolson.

Miller, J. H. 1982: The Communist Party: Trends and Problems. In A. Brown and M. Kaser (eds), *Soviet Policy for the 1980s*. London. Macmillan.

Mills, C. Wright. 1960: *The Causes of World War III*. New York: Ballantine Books.

Moore, R. 1977: Migrants and the Class Structure of Western Europe. In R. Scase (ed.), *Industrial Society: Class, Cleavage and Control*. London: Allen & Unwin.

Mouzelis, N. 1978: *Modern Greece: Facets of Underdevelopment*. London: Macmillan.

Newby, H. 1977: Paternalism and Capitalism. In R. Scase (ed.), *Industrial Society: Class, Cleavage and Control*. London: Allen & Unwin.

Nichols, T. 1975: The 'Socialism' of Management: Some Comments on the New Human Relations. *Sociological Review*. (vol. 23, no. 2).

Noble, T. 1981: *Structure and Change in Modern Britain*. London: Batsford.

Nove, A. 1969: *An Economic History of the USSR*. London: Allen Lane.

Oakley, A. 1972: *Sex, Gender and Society*. London: Temple Smith.

Oakley, A. 1981: *Subject Women*. Oxford: Martin Robertson.

OECD. 1984a: *Economic Outlook*, no. 36. Paris: OECD.

OECD. 1984b: *Quarterly Labourforce Statistics*, no. 4 Paris: OECD.

Pahl, R. E. 1984: *Divisions of Labour*. Oxford: Basil Blackwell.

Parkin, F. 1971: *Class Inequality and Political Order*. London: MacGibbon & Kee.

Parkin, F. 1979: *Marxism and Class Theory*. London: Tavistock Publications.

Poulantzas, N. 1972: *Political Power and Social Classes*. London: New Left Books.

Poulantzas, N. 1975: *Social Classes in Contemporary Capitalism*. London: New Left Books.

Pravda, A. 1979: Industrial Workers: Patterns of Dissent, Opposition and Accommodation. In R. L. Tökés (ed.), *Opposition in Eastern Europe*. London: Macmillan.

Pryce, K. 1979: *Endless Pressure: A Study of West Indian Life-Styles in Bristol*. Harmondsworth: Penguin Books.

Rakovski, M. 1978: *Towards an East European Marxism*. London: Allison & Busby.

Reed, J. 1960: *Ten Days that Shook the World*. New York: Vintage Books.

Reid, I. 1981: *Social Class Differences in Britain*. (Second edition.) London: Grant McIntyre.

Reports by the Experience and Future Discussion Group (DIP) Warsaw. 1981: *Poland: The State of the Republic*. London: Pluto Press.

Richardson, J. and Henning, R. (eds) 1984: *Unemployment: Policy Responses of Western Democracies*. London: Sage.

Rius 1976: *Marx for Beginners*. London: Writers and Readers Publishing Cooperative.

Salaman, G. 1981: *Class and the Corporation*. London: Fontana.

Sawyer, M. 1976: *Income Distribution in the OECD Countries*. Paris: OECD.

Scase, R. 1977: *Social Democracy in Capitalist Society*. London: Croom Helm.

Scase, R. (ed.) 1980: *The State in Western Europe*. London: Croom Helm.

Scase, R. 1983: Why Sweden has Elected a Radical Government. *Political Quarterly*, 54 (1) (January–March).

Scase, R. and Goffee, R. 1980: *The Real World of the Small Business Owner*. London: Croom Helm.

Scase, R. and Goffee, R. 1982: *The Entrepreneurial Middle Class*. London: Croom Helm.

Schumacher, E. 1973: *Small is Beautiful*. London: Blond & Briggs.

Scott, J. 1979: *Corporations, Classes and Capitalism*. London: Hutchinson.

Seabrook, J. 1982: *Unemployment*. London: Quarter Books.

Shaw, M. (ed.) 1984: *War, State and Society*. London: Macmillan.

Sik, O. 1976: *The Third Way: Marxist-Leninist Theory and Modern Industrial Society*. (Translated by Marian Sling.) London: Wildwood House.

Skocpol, T. 1979: *States and Social Revolutions: A Comparative Analysis of France, Russia and China*. Cambridge: Cambridge University Press.

Smith, A. 1910: *The Wealth of Nations* (2 vols). London: Dent.

Smith, D. 1977: *Racial Disadvantage in Britain*. Harmondsworth: Penguin Books.

Stephens, J. 1979: *The Transition from Capitalism to Socialism*. London: Macmillan.

Stonier, T. 1983: *The Wealth of Information*. London: Methuen.

Strinati, S. 1982: *Capitalism, the State and Industrial Relations*. London: Croom Helm.

Szelenyi, I. 1983: *Urban Inequalities under State Socialism*. Oxford: Oxford University Press.

Taylor, F. W. 1947: *Scientific Management*. New York: Harper & Row.

Thompson, E. P. 1982: Time, Work-Discipline, and Industrial Capitalism. In A. Giddens and D. Held (eds), *Classes, Power and Conflict*. London: Macmillan.

Thompson, K. 1976: *Auguste Comte: The Foundation of Sociology*. London: Nelson.

Toffler, A. 1980: *The Third Wave*. London: Collins.

Tökés, R. L. (ed.) 1979: *Opposition in Eastern Europe*. London: Macmillan.

Touraine, A. 1983: *Solidarity: Analysis of a Social Movement, Poland 1980-81*. Cambridge: Cambridge University Press.

Urry, J. 1981: *The Anatomy of Capitalist Societies*. London: Methuen.

Utton, M. 1970: *Industrial Concentration*. Harmondsworth: Penguin Books.

Uusitalo, H. 1975: *Income and Welfare: A Study of Income as a Component of Welfare in the Scandinavian Countries in the 1970s*. Helsinki: Research Group for Comparative Sociology.

Walker, C. R. 1957: *Towards the Automatic Factory*. New Haven: Yale University Press.

Weber, M. 1930: *The Protestant Ethic and the Spirit of Capitalism*. London: Unwin University Books.

Weber, M. 1948: Bureaucracy. In H. Gerth and C. W. Mills (eds) *From Max Weber: Essays in Sociology*. London: Routledge & Kegan Paul.

Weber, M. 1964: *The Theory of Social and Economic Organisation*. Glencoe, Ill.: The Free Press.

Weber, M. 1978: *Selections in Translation*. (Edited by W. G. Runciman and translated by E. Matthews.) Cambridge: Cambridge University Press.

Westergaard, J. and Resler, H. 1975: *Class in a Capitalist Society*. London: Heinemann.

Westoby, A. 1981: *Communism since World War II*. Brighton: Harvester.

Wilkinson, B. 1983: *The Shopfloor Politics of New Technology*. London: Heinemann.

Williams, B. 1984: Shorter Hours. In *Three Banks Review*, no. 143.

Wilson Committee. 1979: *The Financing of Small Firms*. Cmnd 7503. London: HMSO.

Winkler, J. 1977: The Corporatist Economy: Theory and Administration. In R. Scase (ed.), *Industrial Society: Class, Cleavage and Control*. London: Allen & Unwin.

Wood, S. (ed.) 1982: *The Degradation of Work?* London: Hutchinson.

Yanowitch, M. 1977: *Social and Economic Inequality in the Soviet Union*. London: Martin Robertson.

Yanowitch, M. and Fisher, W. A. (eds) 1973: *Social Stratification and Mobility in the USSR*. White Plains, N.Y.: Int. Arts and Sciences Press.

Zagorski, K. 1974: *Changes of the Socio-Occupational Mobility in Poland*. Jablonna: Central Statistical Office.

Zauberman, A. 1964: *Industrial Progress in Poland, Czechoslovakia and East Germany 1937-62*. London: Oxford University Press.

Index